MW00445494

Praise for
HOW TO WALK
INTO A ROOM

"In a time when so many of us have lost old pathways of belonging, Emily meets us in the middle of our anxiety and uncertainty with practical wisdom, gentle companionship, and good questions. If you are in a season of evolution, this book is so much more than a framework for discernment; it is a map for loving God, loving ourselves, and loving our world right in the midst of our uncharted places."

—Sarah Bessey, *New York Times* bestselling
author of *A Rhythm of Prayer*

"With the wisdom of a listener and the language of a poet, Emily P. Freeman helps us discern where our lives call for adjustments and how to move forward in peace. Generous and vulnerable, *How to Walk into a Room* seals Freeman's fate as one of the great spiritual guides of our time."

—Shannan Martin, author of *Start with Hello*
and *The Ministry of Ordinary Places*

"Emily P. Freeman offers a compassionate road map to managing these internal tensions in order to live a more meaningful and value-aligned life."

—Dr. Meg Arroll, author of *Tiny Traumas*

"Level-headed . . . wise and compassionate resource for those looking to begin their next chapter."

—*Publisher's Weekly*

How
to Walk
into a
Room

The Art of Knowing When to Stay
and When to Walk Away

EMILY P. FREEMAN

HARPERONE
An Imprint of HarperCollinsPublishers

FIRST EDITION

Designed by Janet Evans-Scanlon

Library of Congress Cataloging-in-Publication Data has been applied for.

ISBN 978-0-06-332882-2

24 25 26 27 28 LBC 5 4 3 2 1

To Ava, Stella, and Luke,
This one was always for you.

For everything there is a season and a
time for every matter under heaven:

a time to be born and a time to die;

a time to plant and a time to pluck up
what is planted;

a time to kill and a time to heal;

a time to break down and a time to
build up;

a time to weep and a time to laugh;

a time to mourn and a time to dance;

a time to throw away stones and a time
to gather stones together;

a time to embrace and a time to refrain
from embracing;

a time to seek and a time to lose;

a time to keep and a time to throw away;

a time to tear and a time to sew;

a time to keep silent and a time to speak;

a time to love and a time to hate;

a time for war and a time for peace.

ECCLESIASTES 3:1–8

Contents

Part 1

ON LEAVING:

How to Walk out of a Room

Shirley Temple leaves Hollywood at age twenty-two, to later become a US ambassador. The Beatles play their last performance together in 1969, announcing their breakup a few years later. Richard Nixon resigns from office in 1974. Michael Jordan retires from basketball (all three times). Oprah Winfrey ends her talk show after twenty years. Steve Carell leaves the cast of *The Office* before the series finishes. The Duke and Duchess of Sussex step down from their roles as senior working royals and move to California. Simone Biles pulls out of the team gymnastics competition on live TV at the 2021 Olympics. Beth Moore leaves the Southern Baptist Convention.

These exits, while vastly different in context, background, scope, and impact, all have something in common: they happened publicly. Either we've read about them in the history books or we've seen the headlines, the press conferences, or the prime-time specials announcing them, and we have our opinions, impressions, outrage, and nostalgia to show for it. Some of these exits were forced, some anticipated, some discerned. But in all of them, we are not privy to the conversations, struggles, questions, confusions, acceptance, excitement, full stories, or decisions that took place behind the scenes. We don't get to watch the discernment process in action. And yet we all walk through exits and endings throughout our lives. This book is about what happens in the rooms be-

hind our own closed doors, behind the scenes and be-
neath the surface that leads up to our own endings,
leavings, and goodbyes.

Whether it's a job, a friendship, a community, a house, or
a habit, there are a million reasons why it may be difficult
to imagine leaving, especially if that space, relationship, or
community has meant a lot to you. If you're in a season of
life when you're considering making a change, here are a
few questions you might be asking yourself:

Should I stay or is it time to leave?

Am I allowed to even ask that question?

How bad does something have to be before I can let it go?

What if I helped to build this place?

What if this place built me?

What if I stay and nothing changes?

What if I leave and everything falls apart?

Our whole life is like a house, and every commitment,
community, role, and relationship is like a room. At some
point we'll find ourselves walking into new rooms, leav-
ing old rooms, being locked out of other rooms, or look-
ing around at familiar rooms and questioning if it's time
to move on. I hope this grounding metaphor of consider-
ing the rooms of our lives can be a helpful way for you to
assess what rooms you're currently in, what rooms it
might be time to change or leave, and what new rooms
might be waiting for you.

As we make these kinds of decisions, we're usually
looking for clarity and certainty. But the kind of clarity

we want isn't the kind we get from lists, books, or formulas. Most things we know, we didn't learn in a classroom. We tend to doubt this kind of knowing because we cannot annotate, cross-reference, footnote, or cite it. We can't explain it, diagram it, or defend it in a court of law. When something comes into our lives—a doubt, a restlessness, a sense that it's time to make a change—and we find it difficult to put into words, or we try to express it and are dismissed or ignored, then it makes sense we would begin to outsource our confidence.

Of course we don't know everything. But I agree with poet Pádraig Ó Tuama, who says, "We might know more than we know we know."[1] I'm still learning this for myself. My hope for you is that this book will be the beginning of the end of your subconscious compulsion to trust everyone else more than you trust yourself, not as a replacement for God or community but in loving partnership with them, as one who has voice, as one who belongs, as one who can be trusted.

As a spiritual director, I spend a lot of time listening to people ask questions about their lives. Most of my training has been less about learning how to listen and more about unlearning all the toxic ways we usually listen: to advise, to one-up, to help. My role is not to give an answer but to hold space for people to listen to their life in the presence of God, to watch for small or large signs of hope, direction, clarity, and light.

It's likely that in whatever you are facing, you are

looking for direction and relief. I hope the stories, questions, practices, and prayers in this book provide that for you. But I also think it's worth noting that the discernment process is not necessarily about asking a question and coming out with a clear answer. Discernment is a formation process necessary to grow our faith, to teach us what it means to hear God, and to draw us into community. It's about becoming wholehearted people and leading confidently from that space. All of this is part of our formation: mind, body, and spirit.

In the spiritual direction room, questions are always allowed. As we journey together through these pages, I hope this book will be that kind of room for you. No question is off-limits. No wondering is too big or too small. You are allowed to show up fully, to rage, to laugh, to weep. You are even allowed to hide, avoid, defer, or protect yourself. There is no agenda here.

In this first part, we'll take inventory of the rooms in your life, paying particular attention to the ones you may be questioning (or the ones that are questioning you). Once you're aware of the rooms in question I'll serve as a companion for you along the way, offering practices to engage in and questions to consider as you begin to clarify your next move.

In part 2, we'll enter the hallway, confronting some

commonly held misconceptions about staying and leaving. We'll consider what to bring with you when you exit a room and what to leave behind, and we'll examine your narratives about answers, peace, readiness, timeliness, and closure.

Finally, in part 3, we'll explore how to walk into a new room as the person you most fully are: as a leader, a listener, and a friend.

Engaging in this process of discernment together is kind of like turning on the lights. As you begin to look at the rooms that have made you and the ones in the making, you may sense that turning on an overhead light or flinging open the drapes feels like too much, too soon. That's okay. My prayer for you is that this process feels less like the bright light of fluorescent bulbs and more like the gradual flicker of lighting a candle. A flame that sparks to life and softly grows, offering a warm circle of light to sit within.

Along the way, I'll bring you with me into my own discernment process as I've left some significant rooms in my life. I'll share a lot of myself, perhaps more than I've ever shared in print before. But my profound hope is that in reading some of my story, you'll be accompanied on your own. Parts of my own stories of leaving that I'll share are so common, so familiar to so many people, that I hesitate to write about them because they almost feel cliché. But clichés are, by definition, phrases that are overused and taken so far away from their intended context that they lose all meaning and impact. Our work, then, is to put these experiences back into context, to fill in the missing parts and the general pieces with nuance, specificity, and humanity. A life experience cannot be cliché. We bring so much of ourselves into the rooms we enter. And when it's time to leave, we may leave so much of ourselves behind. I'll work to walk with you on purpose, to point to some corners you may have forgotten or ignored, but also to call out to the light that falls through the windows of these rooms, imperfect as they are. Books aren't meant to do everything—something authors sometimes forget as we're writing. I hope you can forgive me if I try to stretch the metaphor too far. Trust yourself to know which parts you need and which parts you can leave behind.

Maybe you need someone to tell you that no matter how much you wanted something, prayed for something, or worked hard to get it, if the room no longer seems to fit, it's good to begin to explore why. You are allowed to ask questions. You are allowed to reconsider. You are allowed to look around and to look again. I'm genuine in my desire to not tell you exactly what that ought to look like, what might come of it, or what you ought to do next. But what I can do is offer a framework for your questions and an arrow for your next right thing. No matter what questions you find yourself holding on to today—plans to be made, answers to be given, relationships to be tended, mysteries begging to be solved—perhaps this reminder is enough direction as we get started. As we begin to hold space for this conversation, you are allowed to ask your questions, and I hope you'll allow me to ask mine.

"One day our kids will get married in this room." I say this to my friend Anna with a casual confidence as we both look straight ahead, leaning against opposite sides of the doorframe, taking in the scene. Winter light of a January morning spills into the large rectangular room, mirroring the new-beginning kind of hope I feel.

It's 2019, and her oldest is a year older than my twins, all of them in high school, and we both have sons in middle school. She nods in agreement; of course all our kids will be married in this room. This is our church and here is her sanctuary, even though it doesn't look much like a sanctuary yet.

Today we've gathered to work. Straight ahead, on the makeshift stage, friends stand on scaffolding and impossibly tall ladders, working to stain plywood panels, hands protected by blue latex gloves. To our right, several large canvas banners lie flat on the low-pile carpeted floor, waiting to be pulled across metal framing bars, signs to hang near the children's classrooms. The smell of fresh wood, new paint, and expectation linger in the air, with sawhorses and drop cloths where chairs will soon be.

It's been years since this traditional-style sanctuary

held pews, as the congregation that owned this building before us was known more for fog machines than liturgy, and we've been working every weekend to make this old new space our own, wanting the vibe to reflect our contemplative, artistic, thoughtful community. We've only owned this seventy-year-old building for a handful of weeks, but the work of shaping it is well underway. The room itself is lovely even on this rainy morning, tall windows bringing in light on either side, casting warm undertones on everyone and everything and every idea of the future.

We've all contributed to the building fund so that we could move from the warehouse where the congregation had been meeting for years to this new-to-us building with room to grow. I proudly wrote a large check at the end of the year to go toward the purchase price and was glad to do so.

Standing with Anna at the back entrance to the sanctuary, taking a short break from our work, considering our church and our future, I imagine my kids on their wedding days, try to picture our lives in this space—the prayers wombed by the walls, the light these windows will allow, the way the exposed brick holds a sacred boundary for the work of the people, the confession of the creeds, the celebration of baptisms, the sorrow of funerals, the familiarity of Sunday morning rituals. Of course it's just a building. But it's also a promise. *Here is a space where you belong,* it says. *Here is a room that will bear witness to your continued becoming, your confession, your life, and your faith. Here is your future, your home.*

Standing in my sweatpants, nodding along with Anna, working alongside dear friends and pastors with the giddy energy that comes from inhabiting a new space, I couldn't have imagined that nearly one year from that very day, we would walk out of this room for the last time. I couldn't have imagined willingly leaving a place I loved so much. I couldn't have imagined then that in order to hold on to my faith, I would have to let go of my church.

Rooms and Scripts

Sometimes what we're born into suits us just fine . . .
but if you're feeling called to explore a life outside the
boundaries you inherited . . . don't let old stories
stand in your way.

—JAMES VAN DER BEEK

The 10,000-hour rule states that "it takes 10,000 hours of intensive practice to achieve mastery of complex skills and materials." This idea was popularized by Malcolm Gladwell in his bestselling book *Outliers* and was purportedly based on a study co-authored by Anders Ericsson, a professor of psychology at Florida State University.

If 10,000 hours is what it takes to become an expert at a skill, then the whole world would have a master's degree in leaving, starting over, and saying goodbye. We've been doing these things our whole lives. By now we should all be experts at knowing when it's time to go and when it's time to stay. But what if the way we've been practicing isn't resulting in mastery? We've done our 10,000 hours and then some, but our practice is weary and cautious. We've left rooms and entered new ones, but we often feel brokenhearted, cynical, and lonely. We're wondering if the choices we have made (or plan to make) are good ones.

Since the release of *Outliers*, Anders Ericsson has pointed out there is one key element of the 10,000-hour rule that Gladwell left out: *the importance of how good the student's teacher is.*[1] To call ourselves experts, 10,000 hours of practice isn't enough for us. What if we're practicing with bad technique? Incorrect form? Misguided narratives? Doing something for 10,000 hours will definitely lead to transformation. But the question is: *What kind?*

We've been navigating arrivals and departures our whole lives. When we take this 10,000-hour concept and apply it to the ways in which we decide to stay or go, are we being formed toward peace, hope, love, or wholeheartedness? Or is our practice leading to bitterness, rage, division, or regret? Are we becoming more fully ourselves in the process? Or are we working to appease other people and losing ourselves along the way?

These are things we've been forced to practice but never properly learned: how to leave, how to wait, and how to start again. In an effort to make it through, some have left too soon, walking all the way out, leaving everything behind without a look back. Others left on time but didn't have a framework for reflection or support to know how to walk into the rooms waiting for them. Still others were forced to leave even though they wanted to stay and are left asking *What now?* And then there are those who stayed but are wondering if they should have left a long time ago.

When it comes to making big decisions about when to stay or go, we've all had a lot of practice. But we still question our place and wonder if we're doing this right. And so we walk along the narrow edge between knowing and unknowing, where our questions open doors to uncertainties about belonging and identity. This is the threshold where we now stand: Is it time to stay or is it time to walk away? Discerning the answer begins with identifying the rooms of our lives.

Moments after I was born, my dad snapped a photo of me, blurry, bloody, and wailing with a shock of black hair. My mom knows for sure it's me because when my sister was born three years before me, they didn't allow anyone into the delivery room, much less someone holding a camera. I've been familiar with this image my whole life, but the emotion I feel upon seeing it again surprises me.

The image itself is discolored in one corner, partially because it was color film in the late 1970s but also possibly from water damage in one of the basements where it likely spent most of the last forty years. You can see the light of a Friday morning sun spilling into the hospital room, a faceless doctor with green latex gloves gripping my small, red body, holding me up to the camera.

This was the room I entered into first, the room where my life on Earth began, where the light came through the window, where the strange, gloved hands held my body first. Just me, my mother, that faceless doctor, and my dad behind the camera. I don't have words for seeing that photo again later in my life, though it elicits something primal in me: *There it is. Evidence of my arrival.* But knowing I was born in a room with a window feels like a gift for which I didn't know to ask.

I had no more control over my arrival than you did at your own moment of birth. Maybe you came in through the bathwater of a midwife's tub or onto the unsuspecting back seat of a frantically moving car or in a regular hospital room with light blue cinder-block walls. Maybe you arrived upon a sterile table beneath surgical lights, or maybe your first room wasn't a room at all but an open-air yard or a subway station. Maybe your birth story has been written about or reported on because it was so extraordinary.

I consider myself one of the lucky ones to have a photo to study at all. You might not know much about the day of your birth. Perhaps it's something you have wondered about or wish you could learn about. If you were born at a time when cameras (or partners, for that matter) were not allowed in the delivery room, then this would not be available to you. If you arrived into the world to a family who didn't take photos, couldn't afford a camera, or didn't think to document such things; if you are a child of adoption; if your birth was traumatic or riddled with complication or cloaked in mystery and secrets, then you may have given up trying to find photographic evidence of the day you were born. You may not even be sure of your true birthday.

But the fact remains that there was a real day you were born, even if known only to God. Even if there is no photo to point to or room to study or field to learn from or voice to bear witness. There was a time in history when you began your becoming, and there was a space into which you entered for the very first time. When you did, you arrived with a deep, full first breath of life, taking in any air the room had to offer. Your wailing that day was not an alarm; it was a celebration.

Hello, small you. The world is different now that you've arrived. The day you were born, the place where it happened, and the people who were there were all outside of your control. It was your first room.

After the first room, our lives consist of a colorful dance of entering and leaving rooms, sometimes with joy—a moving-up ceremony into kindergarten, wrapping up a sports season, graduation from high school, and later events like marriages, births, and retirements. The confetti falls and the music plays and we experience the mixed feelings of pride or moving on with confidence, combined with a warm kind of sadness that our time in that room has come to an end. We gather up our keepsakes, tuck them deep away, and move on to other rooms as planned.

Other times we leave rooms in turmoil, heartbreak, and loneliness, wishing it didn't have to be this way but knowing that it's time. Sometimes just showing up and telling the truth will get us kicked right out of a room we've been in all our lives, with no questions allowed. And we're left standing in a hallway with nowhere to go, hands empty, heart broken, and accusations hanging in the air. These liminal hallways might be the most complicated to talk about: nonspaces that aren't rooms at all, without clear beginnings or endings. (We'll spend more time addressing these hallways in part 2.)

When things end, our first assumption may be that something went wrong. But what if, finally, something has gone magnificently right? Perhaps the right/wrong binary is no longer helpful. Perhaps the room was blue and now we need green. And we needed blue for quite some time—it nourished and cared for us; blue was a comfort

15 ▶

and a joy, a soft place to rest and a safe place to be ourselves. But now blue feels cold, is making us queasy, and we long for a different shade, or no shade at all. Maybe we don't know why; maybe there isn't a discernible reason; maybe we'll never know at all. Sometimes there is no story. Sometimes there is just our lives, carrying on without explanation or understanding, daily tasks mixed up with big decisions, milestones marked after the fact.

There are countless rooms we all inhabit and countless reasons why we might consider leaving them. Maybe you're considering physically leaving your current home to be closer to family, to accept a new job, or to accommodate a new family member. Maybe you need to move because of marriage, remarriage, divorce, retirement, or the death of someone you love. Maybe you're leaving a job to stay home with kids or parents, because you're changing your vocation, you're following a partner, you need to make more money, you're starting a business, you've been fired, let go, laid off, or you've simply changed your mind. Maybe you're grieving a loss you didn't choose, the loss of love or friendship because of death, politics, religion, miscommunication, or you're simply beginning a new season of life.

This is a book about those rooms and hallways, a book of naming and discovering what happens in these rooms, how to discern when it's time to go and when it's good to stay. Because we know some rooms are for us and some rooms are not for us. It gets tricky, though, when a room where we once belonged isn't a room for us anymore.

Since our first room, we've been moving to the healthy, human rhythm of leaving rooms and finding new ones. This is how it always is and how it's supposed to be. Then why do we have so many questions? Why is it so difficult to accept the change, or to be the one to leave a room in the first place? How can we know when it's time to stay or go? Who will teach us how to leave well and how to say goodbye? Staying and leaving is how it's supposed to be. You're not the exception. There isn't something wrong with you when you feel as if you no longer belong. But this feeling alone may not be telling you the whole story. It could mean it's time to look beneath the surface at the room you're in and the script it carries.

For one week twice a year, I make my way from my home in North Carolina to Wichita, Kansas, in order to serve as a residency lecturer at a small liberal arts university. I almost said no to this job because I couldn't imagine a world where I was qualified to serve in a room alongside men who graduated from Yale and Princeton. Even though no one was asking me to be a Very Intelligent Theologian, I was intimidated all the same and almost talked myself out of saying yes. But I did say yes, because there's a way of knowing you don't only learn in school, and it seemed they wanted what they saw of God as revealed through my unique personality.

As a spiritual director and co-lecturer, it's my job and my honor to hold space for students earning their master's degrees in spiritual formation and leadership. It isn't explicitly stated anywhere on a contract, but one of my self-appointed jobs during these weeklong residencies is to *get them in the room*. This may seem small, especially in the world of academia, filled with lectures in theology and dynamic group conversation. But how we walk into a room is worth some exploration, as it affects everything that happens there. There are as many ways to walk into a room as there are people in that room. There are also as many ways to walk out.

When it comes to the rooms we enter throughout our lives, it looks like we're all doing the same thing. There is generally one way in, sometimes multiple doors from a hallway, a front yard, a parking lot, or a connecting room. There may have been a set time for everyone to arrive at the house, the place of worship, the office, the auditorium, the theater, the classroom, the courtroom, or the gym. It's true that we may arrive at the same time of day, the same day of the year, the same space, the same zip code, gathering under the same roof. But the mistake we make is to assume we're all in the same room. Physically, this may be true. But there are entire stories and lifetimes that have been lived up to this moment. There are narratives at play and relational challenges at work and memory upon memory running for free just beneath the surface. We usually aren't aware of that. But it's a reality we would do well to keep in mind, because that reality will play out in one way or another. When it does, we'll be deeply confused if we started out believing that we were in the same room as everyone else when in fact we were not. How we're formed informs how we walk into rooms.

For the entire week during these graduate residencies, the groups meet in a Catholic retreat center (though we are not a Catholic group) in one large, windowless room. I've spent many hours in this room, as both a student and a facilitator-lecturer. On the first day of residency with a new group of thirty students, I always pay attention to *how* they walk into the room. I know that by the end of the week, some of them will have sat in the same seat every day, coming in early to leave a notebook or a jacket at their place to save it. I know that some students will have to stand up in the back just before lunch because sitting for an entire morning listening to teaching, no matter how riveting, is too much for their bodies to endure, because of either their personality, a past injury, a chronic pain, or simple discomfort. I know that for at least one night during the week this retreat room will become a makeshift game room, where we'll gather wearing sweatshirts and pass around snacks, shout, and compete through charades or fishbowl. But by the next morning, we'll be back to reverential silence, transformed into students and contemplatives again.

I know the students will walk out of this room at the end of the week with a shared experience, but not the *same* experience. They'll have some overlapping memories as well as notebooks or laptops filled with notes and quotes and references for the papers they'll have to write. When they walk out, the experience they take with them depends on the experience they brought with them, including their (positive, negative, or neutral) impressions of retreat centers, Catholicism, icons, Kansas, windowless rooms, the smell of coffee, their expectations of what grad school should be like. Their experience of the week will be influenced by their childhood, their gender, their particular faith tradition, how comfortable they are having discourse with others who may disagree with them, their experience of small groups, or whether or not I, or any of the other teachers, remind them of someone they know from their past. The way they walk into the room is informed by what was happening in the last room they left—if they have a struggling child at home, a big deadline looming at work, a rift in a friendship that will be waiting for them when they return. How we're formed informs how we walk into rooms. And how we walk into rooms has an impact on what happens once we get there.

In her book *The Art of Gathering*, author and trained facilitator Priya Parker writes that all rooms come with scripts. Every room has a story, but the story is different depending on who you are and what room you're in. It's one reason why we can all be in the same room but not have the same experience of that room.

Before we can discern if it's time to leave a room, it's important to name the scripts that come with the rooms we're currently in. These scripts bear weight, as they outline for us acceptable patterns of behavior in rooms, expected ways of being within their walls, as well as the nuance of our own experiences in the rooms.

Imagine for a moment all the various rooms with which we may be familiar: rooms of religion, politics, education, athletics, health care, business, family. And then imagine all the various scripts, or expected and accepted behaviors, that may accompany these rooms. Parts of the scripts will be the same for all of us. In the college classroom, the script may include (but is not limited to) respecting dialogue, debate, reason, order, lecture, and learning. The preschool classroom has a more colorful script, with space for play, creativity, and naps.

The room of athletics places a high value on pushing through, physical fitness, teamwork, conditioning, practice, and winning. Politics has its own set of rules, loyalties, and expectations, similar to the room of entrepreneurship with its hustle and strategy scripts. Some rooms of faith place a high value on silence and contemplation, and this is the script you're expected to follow, while others embrace celebratory dancing and shouting in the aisles. Both rooms of faith, both wildly different scripts.

Rooms may carry different scripts for each of us, depending on our family of origin and particular life experience. These rooms are unique, informed by our social location, racial identity, religious affiliation, and educational background. We have scripts we memorize from our youngest days, maybe even things no one ever said but we just know because they are baked into our own family system. Your family script consists of particular beats, like *We don't ask Grandpa about his time in combat* or *When they repeat that story for the seventy-fifth time, our role is to laugh*. Your people may be the calorie counters, the short fusers, the secret keepers, the grudge holders. Maybe they are the nice ones, the quiet ones, the religious ones, the fun ones, the dependable ones, or the dysfunctional ones. Perhaps the scripts you were handed from the places where you grew up are ones that fit your personality quite well. Or maybe you've been going off script your whole life.

If life were a house, then every room would hold a story. Think of those rooms where you've felt most fully, freely, fantastically yourself. The luckiest among us can point to an early room of our life. For me, it's summer morning light spilling onto the orangey hardwood floors of my childhood bedroom, sister nearby, Ivy the cat sleeping on the bed. We would arrange makeshift houses for Barbies with a mix of store-bought doll furniture and household items: a thin floral washcloth as an area rug, a tiny fake plant as a Barbie ficus tree, a plastic pink sofa-and-chair set we got for Christmas. In that Columbus, Indiana, bedroom I shared with my sister—the one without doors on the room or the closet—we shared a bed, and I slept against the wall so I wouldn't fall out in the middle of the night. That was a room where I felt fully myself.

Since then there have been other rooms where I've felt that sense of wholeness and peace. Any room where I get to teach or to gather with a small group of people over a long period of time, to relate and learn with and from them, that's a room where I feel like I belong. In a room filled with writers and makers, people who see the threads beneath the obvious, who connect dots others can't always see, that's another room I'm drawn to. When I'm in the spiritual-direction chair, bearing witness to the inner life of another, holding space for them while they name the visible and invisible things, looking for signs of God, this is when I feel most fully myself. A particularly ordinary day comes to mind: when my husband, John, and our three kids, all in grade school at the time, watched the snow fall outside our living room window, the kids exhausted from outside play, holding mugs of hot chocolate, cartoons on in the background. In this, I recognize another room where I have belonged and helped to create belonging for those I love.

When you look over your life, you can hopefully point to some rooms (or at least corners of rooms) where you have felt most fully yourself, where your mind, heart, and body have felt integrated and aligned. Where you can sit down—not only on the outside but also on the inside—and know you have a place at the table.

Of course not all rooms are like this. I have encountered rooms where I merely had to step one foot inside to realize fast that this was not a room for me. I was part of a committee once that I thought would be a good fit. I loved what they stood for and who they supported. But as soon as I started sharing my ideas and perspective, I knew quickly that my words weren't welcome there. Thankfully I had the wisdom to say my thank-yous and goodbyes, leaving that room for good. It wasn't a bad room, but it wasn't a room for me.

If you're regularly in the minority in a room, you may be more accustomed than most to reading the rooms you're in to determine if your voice and presence are welcome in that space, like if you're the only BIPOC (Black, Indigenous, or other person of color) in your workplace or the only woman in a room of men. If you're an intern in a boardroom of professionals, a single person in a group of couples, or a Deaf student in a hearing classroom, then you have likely developed keen skills of observation and discernment. If you're consistently "the only" in a space, no one needs to teach you to read the rooms you're in, as you've been doing this all your life.

Perhaps the most difficult decisions we make about the various rooms of our lives are ones about the rooms we love and that have loved us. These are spaces we've memorized and could navigate in the dark without stubbing one toe. We know the people; they know us. We know the processes and the rules, both spoken and unspoken. These are the rooms where we've tucked our socked feet beneath us on the sofa, stayed up late into the night, relating and laughing and listening with compassion.

But then something happens: a rift, a realization, a shift, a turn. Maybe the shift is external, a decision someone else makes that affects you, or maybe it's an internal one. And you begin to feel less at home in that room, start to see things you hadn't seen before: a tear in the wallpaper, a broken table leg. You love this room, and your instinct is to get to work, to fix what needs fixing, to shine it all right up. That could be a good and beautiful move to make. But are you sure it's yours to do? And how can you know?

This is the place where we meet now in these pages, the place of asking ourselves if it's time to roll up our sleeves and stay in this room, loving it back to life, making right what has gone wrong. Or has the time arrived for us to say our goodbyes and make our exit, to thank the space and its inhabitants for the gifts they brought, to leave behind what we must, to pack up what we are able, and to walk out the door?

Point and Call

*Few things can bring about change more effectively
than the right question.*

—J. R. BRIGGS AND MICHAEL E. SMITH,

WHY ASK QUESTIONS?

The railway system in Japan is one of the best in the world,
thanks at least in part to its safety system of pointing and
calling. The train operators have a ritual of pointing at dif-
ferent objects and calling out simple and obvious commands, much
like what a toddler does. But instead of the curious prattle of a child,
these railway workers are performing important professional tasks,
though it may not look that way at first.

They engage all their senses as they point at the signal, stating
out loud, "Signal is green." When the train pulls into the station,
the operator points at the speedometer and calls out the speed. At
the time of departure, the operator points at the clock and calls
out the time. Other members of the staff do similar tasks on the

platform as well. Every detail of the operation of the train is iden-
tified, pointed out, and named out loud using various human
senses. The purpose of the system is to minimize mistakes, and it
works—it reduces workplace errors by up to 85 percent.

"Known in Japanese as *shisa kanko*, pointing and calling works
on the principle of associating one's tasks with physical movements
and vocalizations to prevent errors by 'raising the consciousness lev-
els of workers'—according to the National Institute of Occupa-
tional Safety and Health, Japan. Rather than rely on a worker's eyes
or habit alone, each step in a given task is reinforced physically and
audibly to ensure the step is both complete and accurate."[1]

In his book *Atomic Habits*, James Clear uses this concept of
pointing and calling as the origin for his Habits Scorecard, submit-
ting, "The process of behavior change always starts with aware-
ness."[2] In the same way we can learn from this pointing-and-calling
practice to help shape behavior, we can also use it as a foundational
practice for our inner lives to help inform our decisions.

On a train platform one summer in London, I could have bene-
fited from the increased awareness of pointing and calling. I was
headed to Camden Town for some shopping with my then-fifteen-
year-old twins. Earlier in the day, when John was with us, it was
easy to have one parent lead the way through the crowded streets
while the other one walked in the back. But that afternoon, when
he and our son went one way and the twins and I went the other, I
had to make a decision as a solo parent. Would I walk in front and
lead the way, trusting them to stay close behind? Or would I walk
behind them and call out directions as we went, allowing them to
stay in my line of sight? As we headed down the steps to the Tube,

an image flashed in my mind of them getting on the train without me, doors closing between us, train barreling down the tracks, carrying them away from me. So when we arrived on the platform, my highest priority was to avoid accidentally sending them off on the train alone. I confidently stepped on first, trusting they would step on right behind. But what I failed to take into account was how swift and savvy our fellow travelers would be, local to the area, decidedly not going to miss their train to work, brunch, or home. They pushed and shoved their way in behind me, and when I looked back to check on the twins, the doors were already closing between us, leaving them on the other side of the window. In a flurry of slow-motion activity, more hurried travelers tried to push their way in. Sensing the obstruction, the doors popped open long enough for the twins to scurry in behind me, wide-eyed and breathless.

With the doors beeping and my reflex mom-arm now pulsing from trying to pull them in, the whole thing felt sloppy and dangerous. My heart rate didn't slow again until we were safely off the train, aboveground on Camden High Street, standing side by side ordering gelato. Perhaps we could have avoided those harrowing few seconds if we'd had a train worker on our side that afternoon, pointing and calling every obvious step.

Earlier in my life, this simple, redundant point-and-call practice is one I watched my mom engage in every time we left the house. She would check the stovetop, look at all the knobs, and say out loud, "Off, off, off, off." She did the same thing with the iron and the coffeepot. I think she even unplugged them, and then she would say, "Off, off," for them too. I'm sure I rolled my eyes then, but maybe she was onto something. When our kids were little and we wanted a simple way to connect on a daily basis, we sat at the top of the stairs and each shared our favorite part of the day. This, too, was a way of pointing and calling, of saying out loud together what had happened that day and why it was our favorite, in a way that even the youngest in the family could understand.

There's a spiritual practice called the Daily Examen, which is also a form of pointing and calling. Ignatian spirituality defines it as a technique of prayerful reflection on the events of the day in order to detect God's presence and discern God's direction for us. It's an ancient practice of prayer passed down in the church that can help us see where God is working in our lives every day.

All of these are forms of pointing and calling, a movement that brings our awareness forward. It takes something that is typically subconscious and makes it conscious.

Entering rooms (or deciding to exit them) can feel a lot like boarding trains: frantic, disruptive, panicked. Before we can discern where we're going, it's good to name where we are, every obvious bit of it. We started this work of naming our rooms and the scripts that come with them in the previous chapter. A lack of clarity on where we are in time and space, and the absence of an honest assessment of what's happening now, can add to the frustration and confusion of knowing if it's good to stay or if it's time to move on. Sometimes our emotions work to get our attention by pointing to what's going on beneath the surface. A growing sense of dread, a slow-burning frustration, a short fuse, a tearful encounter—all of these could be evidence that a change is needed. But until we bring them to our awareness, we may not know what the change is. We may either make an unnecessary change too soon, to avoid the discomfort, or hang on way past time.

In the same way those train workers use the simple point-and-call practice to maintain their awareness of their surroundings in order to keep people physically safe, we can point and call on the thresholds of our lives to keep ourselves soulfully grounded in times of potential change. It doesn't mean we have to understand the why behind all of our questions and hesitations. But it does mean we may need to finally point to some obvious things we've always known were there, or call out more hidden things that we wish weren't. Before we make our decision to stay or go based on a script gone wrong or a shattered expectation, it's good to practice pointing and calling. Is it time to leave the room? Or is it time to change the script?

If I had a formula for deciding for sure whether or not it was time to leave a room, I promise I would give it to you (and I would also be a billionaire). What I do have, though, are some rhythms, movements, and practices to accompany you as you discern along your way. Throughout our time together, I'll share these four simple movements in the form of an acronym that embodies the posture with which I approach discernment: *PRAY*. These movements may be practiced alone or in community.

● *Point and call*—Explore the primary rooms of your life (coming up next).

◀ *Remember your path*—Look back before moving ahead (see chapter 4).

○ *Acknowledge presence*—Practice four simple types of prayer for direction (see chapter 6).

▶ *Yield to the arrows*—Establish rhythms and rituals for endings and beginnings (also see chapter 6).

We'll address the last three movements of *PRAY* in later chapters, as noted, but for now, here is where you'll begin your own practice of pointing and calling. We'll return to this practice all along the way, so no need to rush through it. Earlier, you took some time to start to identify the rooms of your life and we'll continue that now as if we're touring a house. It may be helpful to write down your answers as you ask yourself the next three preliminary questions.

What are the primary rooms of my life right now? Remember, a "room" can be a physical room, like a sanctuary, a classroom, a workplace, or a home. It may also be a metaphorical room that includes, but is not limited to, commitments, faith communities, relationships, vocation, a particular town or city, a field of study, or hobbies you engage in. It could also include larger systems or mindsets, like the room of a particular stream of faith, political party, group, or club.

What is my general experience in these rooms? Which rooms are you most drawn to these days? Where do you feel most like yourself? What are the newest rooms or the least familiar? Which rooms are the oldest, the rooms you can navigate with your eyes closed?

Once you've taken a general assessment of the rooms of your life, now we'll turn to the room(s) where you notice a catch, a hesitation, a discomfort, or a question.

Is there a room where I'm considering making a change but I'm not sure what change to make? This is where we'll spend the rest of our time together.

Now that you have a particular room in mind to start with, consider the following additional questions as the first steps in the discernment process. We'll refer to them as The Ten Questions and they are foundational questions for now and for later. Your answers to these questions may come quickly. Or you may not have an answer right away. That's okay. You don't have to show anyone your answers or turn them in. But if you're questioning a room, it's vital that you begin this process as honestly as you are able to at this time, so that you can make a decision in alignment with what's actually true now, not what you wish to be true or what used to be true.

The Ten Questions

1. Did I choose this room or did it choose me?

There is no right or wrong answer, and it could be both. Either way, what was the circumstance surrounding that choice? Are those circumstances still at play? What has changed since you got here and what has stayed the same? If you chose this room, would you choose it again? What would have to be true in order for you to answer yes or no to this first question?

2. What are the corners, sections, people, or parts of this room that I'm avoiding?

In other words, are you hesitant to turn on the lights? Do you find yourself making excuses or concessions for or defending certain aspects of this room? How often? What are these about?

3. What is good and beautiful about this room?

Even the rooms we question may have parts we love. That's why we're still here and why this decision isn't easy. What is working here? What do you love? What would you miss? What are its gifts?

4. Where are the caution flags?

Years ago, my friend Holly Good said to me, "Tiny red flags rarely shrink; they only grow."[3] If you have a sense that something is off, chances are you're right. But not every hesitation, fear, worry, or concern is a red flag, though we may not know that at first.

Let's get specific about the questions you have about this room. What's not working here? It's possible to rush out of a room too soon or stay way too long simply because we've misidentified the color of a flag. This is a point-and-call practice, which means you're noticing but not diagnosing. I've found it helpful to just assume every flag is yellow at first. Unlike stoplights, a yellow flag doesn't automatically turn red. It's a caution flag that invites you to slow down. The work, then, is to discern if a yellow flag is leading to a

32

red flag or if it's merely something to pay attention to and consider where it's coming from. Sometimes it will be clear from the start. Other times you'll need help in the process. When you sense hesitation, point at it and call it yellow for now. What are the yellow flags waving in this room?

5. Is anyone or anything missing from this room? If so, who or what?

Some rooms are exclusive by nature: Congress is a room primarily for elected officials; an all-women's college will not admit male students; an annual luncheon might have only donors as guests. Considering the context and purpose of a particular room, is there someone (or a group of someones) who would make this room better, more informed, more beautiful? Is the exclusion intentional or unintentional? Who used to be here but has now left? Who is entering? Who feels comfortable and who is uncomfortable? This may be most relevant in a room that consists of a group of people, like a program, workplace, school, church, or committee. But even in the room of a one-on-one relationship, consider if there are people missing from your life as a result of this relationship. Who are they? What kind of impact does their absence have on your life?

6. Who has the power in this room?

People and systems can misuse or abuse their power. But power is not only a bad word. We all have varying degrees of power, and we all have the responsibility to use it in ways that uplift, encourage, protect, and advocate for good. Who has the power in this room, and to what degree are they wielding their power? Is it you or someone else? What are they willing to do to keep it? How do they respond when power is threatened? Are the things that aren't working things you have the skills, resources, patience, conviction, and/or calling to change? Or to at least try? Or are the things that aren't working outside of your sphere of influence? It's okay if your answer is "I don't know yet."

7. Who or what will be affected by my decision?

Without a point-and-call practice, we may assume our decision will affect everyone or no one when in reality it's probably somewhere in between. It's good to be as specific as you're able. Who benefits from your presence here, and who, if anyone, will benefit if you leave? Who is struggling with your presence here, and who, if anyone, will struggle when you leave? If you're the one with the power, how will your absence affect the room, the people in the room, and the story this room is telling?

8. To what extent can I be myself in this room?

Do you have to change yourself to such a degree that you don't even recognize yourself in order to inhabit this room? If people who know and love you the most showed up in this space, what questions would they have for you? Would they see a version of you that they recognize? Do you constantly have to censor, edit, or muffle your thoughts, ideas, or opinions?

9. If God is in this room, what is the action of the Divine?

This may take some imaginative discernment. But if God were visibly, physically in this room, what would God be doing? Saying? Not saying? What would be the look on God's face? What posture does God have here? What's held in the sacred silence?

10. Do I want to stay in this room?

If the answer is yes, this is good information to hold for now, bearing in mind it's only one of ten questions. If the answer is no, do you *want* to want to stay? What do you wish you wanted?

If you find yourself answering "I don't know" or "I'm not sure yet" a lot, I have good news for you. You're in the right place, and this is the right book for you. If you go through these questions and the answers come quickly, you may be further along than you think in your discernment process. The rest of this book will help clarify your answers.

Remember, pointing and calling—by answering The Ten Questions—is just one of four primary movements. For example, your answers to question 8 may reveal that you cannot be fully yourself in a room, that you often censor and edit yourself in order to stay there. A yes answer doesn't automatically mean this isn't a room for you. Sometimes we stay in spaces and follow uncomfortable scripts and formalities because we have a greater vision in mind and that vision can only come to be if we're present. So these answers, while informative, are not exhaustive. We're pointing and calling; we're taking it slow.

Notice, not one of these questions asks why, and that is intentional. Why is both an overwhelming and underwhelming question. It's often difficult to name clear reasons for things, but we think if we could just find the reason, then we could change, control, or manipulate the outcome (which is why it's overwhelming). But it's also an underwhelming question, because knowing why doesn't always (sometimes ever) help us to know what to do next.

If you come from a faith background, you may expect a question like "What does God think?" Or "What would God have me do?" While deeply important questions to hold, I have found such questions to be difficult to answer in one movement. If they were questions you had immediate answers for, I bet you wouldn't be reading this book (and I wouldn't be writing it). Instead, pointing and calling by using The Ten Questions can be a way to gather clues and information, to begin to pay attention to the movement of God within and around you as revealed through your thoughts, your body, your heart, your people, your prayers, your sacred texts, and your intuition. Communion with and direction from God is rarely a onetime event. We don't always ask and get an answer. We ask and then we listen, live, love, move, sleep, feel, eat, walk, work, play, and pay attention. The Ten Questions help us to pay attention with intention.

So how do you walk out of a room you still love?

How do you leave a place where you once belonged?

How do you know if you have the influence, the authority, or the stamina to stay put and change the script?

How can you know if it's time to admit that this script is too strong, you are too tired, or your boundaries will not stretch to include what you assume it will take to effect change in this room?

To start, point at the longing, and call it out loud. At least start here. Name what is true as far as you understand it.

Point at the room and call what you see.

Point at the door and call out the fear of walking through it.

Point at the floor and call out the fear of staying put.

Point at the windows and call out the light or the lack of light or the shadowed corners.

Point at the furnishings and call out what's tired, what's changed, and where you feel most at home.

Point at the people and call out both the lies and the dignity. And the loves. And the longings too.

Point at yourself and call out what is most true today.

As you hold your answers (or non-answers) to The Ten Questions, you're going to want some direction one way or another. What we all want is to know what to do next. The rest of this book will serve as an arrow to your next right thing, starting now. When you're discerning if it's time to pause, stay, or walk away, you need a path, a presence, and a practice. But first, you have to identify the type of ending you're potentially facing.

Identify the Ending

Everything has to come to an end, some time.

—L. FRANK BAUM, *THE MARVELOUS LAND OF OZ*

I have a friend who reads the last page of every novel to ensure it ends well. If not, she won't read the book at all. Once I worked through my outrage at what I considered to be the greatest insult to a storyteller that you could possibly inflict (right up there with reading spoilers on the internet or shuffling a carefully curated playlist), I asked her more questions about this practice. Over time, I learned she also records key sports events and only watches them if she knows her team wins. I'd never heard of someone orchestrating their lives in such a way as to only ever watch a winning game or read a happy ending. Where is the mystery, the adventure, the joy and anticipation of not knowing how something ends?

As it turns out, not everyone likes a mystery, and in cases of trauma, neglect, or abandonment, enjoying a surprise is a privilege. My reads-the-last-page-of-every-novel friend was a child of the '80s, like me. We both grew up in a generation with Ronald Reagan as president, looked up to Mary Lou Retton and Michael Jackson, played Atari in our basement, watched major blockbusters like *E.T.* and *The Breakfast Club*, as well as bore awestruck witness to the beginning of MTV and VH1. The most existential and pervasive question in our young minds was "Who shot J.R.?" But there were major tragedies that also marked our childhood, like the *Challenger* explosion in 1986, which killed everyone on board, including a teacher, Christa McAuliffe. I was in second grade and didn't know a lot of the details about the trip. But everyone knew about Christa McAuliffe, who was to become the first ordinary US civilian in space and was about the same age as my mom at the time. I didn't learn about the explosion until hours after it happened, when my older sister told me as we walked home from the bus stop that afternoon. I vaguely remember watching footage of it on the news later that night, a shocking fireball, then a thick split-V cloud of smoke against an unbelievably deep blue sky.

That morning, my friend who likes to read the last page of every novel was also in second grade, but she was living in Florida. Her second-grade classroom was going on an exciting field trip to the Kennedy Space Center to watch the *Challenger* liftoff. She felt the record-breaking cold on that late January morning, saw her own breath share the same air as the shuttle. She watched as the shuttle counted down to liftoff, saw the launch and then the explosion in the sky, not understanding at first why.

Now, as an adult, as I consider her preference to read the last page of a novel so she knows how it ends? Well, that makes a lot more sense.

What kind of ending are you facing? This, too, is a point-and-call practice. It's impossible to talk about potentially leaving a room without talking about endings. Storytellers and scriptwriters know that if you want a universally satisfying ending, then your story needs to have some version of four basic elements: surprise, suspense, transformation, and resolution. Suspense compels and intrigues. Surprise entertains and delights. Transformation inspires and enlivens. Resolution brings peace and closure. It's what we look for without realizing it's what we look for. Some endings are labeled terrible and we may not know why, but it could be that the story lacks one of these key elements.

We all have our narratives about endings. The breakups, the abandonments, the celebrations, the retirements, the relocations, the tragedies. All these throughout our lives have shaped our opinions, beliefs, and ideas about what an ending means, about our role in deciding when something ends, or how appropriate or inappropriate it is to quit, walk away, or change our minds.

When it comes to the rooms where we find ourselves, there are at least three ways we generally exit: with an *anticipated* ending, a *forced* ending, or a *chosen* ending. We may not always be able to differentiate clearly between these types of goodbyes, as they may overlap. But for the most part, these are the broad categories we'll explore.

The first category, *anticipated* goodbyes, includes those endings in which you and everyone around you agree that the time has come for a new season. These endings are things like grade promotions or graduations (the continuation or ending of school), retirement (the end of a particular kind of working life), or a move to a new city, in some cases, or a permanent change of station in the military (anticipated because it happens every two to four years). We accept that these kinds of endings come and go with the seasons and stages of life. Of course we will still have our mixed emotions, our various degrees of happiness and joy, grief and sorrow, when something ends. But the question of whether or not it's time to go is not there simply because these types of exits are ones we accept, expect, mark, celebrate, and communally agree are part of life.

The questions we may carry with anticipated endings are different from the ones we carry when we are, for example, forced out of a room or when we didn't see an ending coming. When an ending is expected, we know it's time to leave the room, and most, if not all, of the people in our lives agree. There may be sadness and grief, but it tends to be mixed with celebration or nostalgia.

What I call a *forced* ending is an exit you didn't want and couldn't plan for. You were fired or let go, released early or voted out, left by a partner, abandoned by a parent or caregiver, or excluded from a previously inclusive group. Even if the neglect or oversight was not intentional on the part of the other person or group of people, here you are, left in a hallway of someone else's choosing. What if you wanted to stay in the room and leaving was not your choice? How can you navigate this very real ending that has no semblance of closure?

Part 2 of this book will offer a framework for making peace with anticipated and forced endings. But for now, we'll focus on the third category: *chosen* endings.

Depending on your cultural and social location, you have your own narratives about leaving a room. If you grew up with strong "We don't ever give up" narratives, then the concept of choosing to quit, leave, or end something may feel foreign or even scary to you. Maybe q-u-i-t was the four-letter word you weren't allowed to say. "We honor our commitments." "We stay loyal to our word." Choosing to leave a room may feel like a betrayal, a shame, an option you do not have. Of course there are some commitments that come with being an adult: the responsibility of parenting, of being a citizen, of having a job, of honoring the dignity of fellow humans.

But so many of the stay-at-any-cost standards we may hold ourselves to come from an ingrained belief that if we leave, quit, or change our mind, then that says something about our character. *Maybe that means I'm flaky or unreliable. Maybe this is a verdict about not just my actions but also my identity: Not only did I quit; I am a "quitter."* Add to that narrative the accolades and praise much of society gives to people who push through, persevere, and stay the course. They are the loyal ones, the dependable ones, the ones who can be trusted.

Post-pandemic, some of these narratives began to shift. According to Bloomberg.com, more than twenty-four million people quit their jobs from April to September in the US during what is now known as the Great Resignation of 2021.[1] Other wealthy nations, including Germany, Japan, and China, witnessed similar trends around the same time, though the circumstances and motivations varied widely both between and within countries. As a result of a viral social media post from a computer developer working in Beijing, known simply as Jeff, young Chinese professionals began trading in their grueling work schedules, choosing instead to "lie flat." This meant they were opting out of the hustle and performance culture that expected a 996 work schedule: 9 a.m. to 9 p.m. six days a week. It became so prevalent that it sparked public condemnation from the president, Xi Jinping.[2] While Jeff's viral social media post of passive resistance was a specific and mostly youthful reaction to a particular system and culture, it demonstrates the power dynamics that are often at play in our decisions about staying in a room or walking into a new one. It also illustrates the gap in narratives between the people in positions of power and the people in the rooms, and what happens when those narratives are challenged. As a result of Jeff's viral post, the state media in China issued strong reprimands against the lying flat movement, and the original post disappeared across multiple social networking platforms.[3]

Here in the United States, the "land of the free and the home of the brave," where self-expression and autonomy are often held higher than loyalty to a group or cause, the opposite narrative may be at play. Those who stay may be viewed as old-school, trapped, or unenlightened, and the ones who leave may be seen as brave and courageous.

It's important to point and call our narratives, the ones about staying and about leaving, the ones shaped by our culture, our family of origin, our own lived experience. Our choices, our ability to make them, and our awareness or unawareness of safety, agency, and autonomy will influence the degree to which we're able to make decisions in the first place.

"Emmy, it's time to go!"

"I'll be right there!"

Our little house on Gladstone Avenue was the first house I knew. Every childhood memory I have up to age twelve is tied to either that house or, four minutes away, the split-level house on Westline Drive where Grandma and Grandpa Morland lived. I had no reason to think we would ever leave the small town that was my whole world. Until we did.

At the end of fourth grade, Dad got a job in Iowa, a six-hour drive from our hometown, away from all of our family, my beloved elementary school, the community pool, the JCPenney department store, the McDonald's where I had my first Happy Meal. A move six hours away from home may as well have been a move to Mars.

The day we were scheduled to leave, we stopped by Grandma's house to say goodbye.

As the adults packed the cooler with sandwiches, tucked cans of Big Red down into the ice, and stared at the highlighted foldout map, I snuck away from the kitchen for a few minutes alone. I needed a moment before climbing into the moving truck and making the trip across half of Indiana and all of Illinois to start fifth grade on the barely west side of the Mississippi River. Just before closing the bathroom door behind me, I looked around the small, windowless room: black porcelain sink; bottles of hair spray, perfume, and mousse standing in a line on the counter; tubes of lipstick and mascara scattered over the surface. I looked down at my socked feet making a light impression on the calico carpet. *I'm right here now. This room doesn't know I'm leaving.*

Barely twelve, I stared at my reflection in the water-spotted mirror, not realizing I was pondering the magic of permanence and the passing of time. I imagined how this whole bathroom would still be here when I walked out of the room and turned off the lights. This mirror would be here when I loaded up in the moving truck and rode away from Columbus. That faucet would be here even when I was not, would pour out water and sit in the dark and bear witness to the morning habits of my beautiful grandma as she got ready for her job at the convalescent center, strands of her long silver hair floating onto the carpet as she brushed it into a low ponytail.

What will they do if I don't come out?

Could I fold myself into the cabinet under the sink, making my home with the dusty bottles of cleaner and the extra toilet paper?

Will I still be a Hoosier even though we won't live in Indiana anymore?

Could I buy myself some time?

Are we going to be okay?

Again, I wouldn't have been able to articulate it then, but I had all the questions we carry when confronted with leaving a space. Negotiating an alternative ending, trying to reason with unreasonable solutions, procrastinating to avoid the inevitable, wondering about my identity and safety.

This leaving was not what I would have chosen. I don't know that my parents would have chosen it either, if they'd had another choice. But when Dad lost his job, he needed a new one, and the profession he was growing into required a relocation. There were no jobs available to him in Columbus, so we had to go.

A year and a half after moving to Iowa, we moved again, this time even farther away, to Columbia, South Carolina, where I would spend middle school and most of high school. By the time I graduated from college, I had moved twice more before settling in Greensboro, North Carolina, where I now live. My narratives of leaving and saying goodbye began in that small bathroom at Grandma's house on Westline Drive and kept forming as time passed. Those narratives have been shaped by many moves, many first days of school, many farewells to friend groups, many hellos to new ones.

By contrast, John and I met and married here in Greensboro, a town where he was born. He lived his whole life in one house, stayed in one school district, never moved until he left for college. After twenty-two years of marriage, we still live here. Now we've brought up our own kids here; two of them already graduated from high school—a second generation of Greensborians.

And so the question of leaving or staying in a relationship, in a job, in a vocation, in a volunteer position, at a church, in a particular town or home—these questions are not all created equal. No two people ever have the same decision to make. If you and I are discerning if it's time for each of us to move across the country, I already have ingrained narratives about what that means. If you've lived in the same place your whole life, so do you. We aren't asking the same questions.

Our experiences of leaving and of being left, of walking away and starting again, and our decisions to do that again depends on so many things, not the least of which is how it went the last time, if there was a last time, and if we've ever vowed there would never be a next time.

How we walk into new rooms often depends on the last rooms we were in and how our time there ended. It also depends on whether our leaving was planned, forced, or chosen. A question of pausing, staying, or walking away is not usually one we ask when everything is fine. Instead, it's one we ask when the room we've been in has changed. Or when we have changed. Or when something has come to our attention that was always there but we didn't see it or it didn't bother us or it meant something different from what it means now. There are a million reasons why we may question if the room we're in is still a room where we belong. I hope you hold this question with tenderness and care, honoring the process of discernment and the caution flags you might be holding as you ask it. But before we explore what it's time for and the various types of questions you might be carrying, it's worth making a statement about what we are and are not talking about.

A few months after she entered her first year of college, my daughter came home with a mysterious pain in her side. After visiting her doctor and running some tests, he sent her home with instructions to call back if the pain got worse. If she started to run a fever, she was to head directly to the emergency room. By 6 p.m. that night, we were in the emergency room, and I was offering moral support in my weird new role as the mom of a fresh adult, where I was still responsible for the medical bills but not allowed to see the medical records without my kid's permission. What a world we live in now!

She sat on the paper-covered exam table nursing a low-grade fever and lots of questions, waiting on the results of a scan with concerns that it might be appendicitis. In the end, they didn't find anything out of the ordinary. All her organs looked fine, all her scans were normal, and they prepared to send us home. As the doctor offered some closing instructions, I asked her what she imagined might be causing the pain.

"The emergency room exists to save lives. We've determined her life is not in danger. Beyond that, you'll need to see your primary care doctor for any further diagnosis and care."

It was a frustrating answer, but she made an important point, and I'll make the opposite one now: This book is not an emergency room; it's more like your primary care doctor. If the room you're in right now is one that requires emergency care, if your life or health is at serious risk, if you're in a situation that requires immediate action, there's no need for nuance, much less an entire book, to guide you through the process. If staying in a room is causing you harm or threatening your life, I hope you have the resources and support you need to get out now.

It may be you don't realize you're in an emergency situation yet. In that case, my sincere prayer is that the discernment process we're entering into here together will show you what you need to know and a door will appear for you to walk through to find help, relief, and healing. For now, we'll assume that you're reasonably safe but standing on a threshold with a question: *Is it time for me to pause, to stay, or to walk away?*

Remember Your Path

The path only unfolds behind us,
our steps themselves laying down the road.

— LYNN UNGAR, "THE PATH"

When the leaves turn inside out, that's when you know there's gonna be a tornado." This was weather wisdom I heard as a child, passed down from great-grandmother to grandmother to aunts and mother to me. I believed every word, thought there was something magical in the leaves that only tornado air could wake up. So I kept an eye on them when our Southern Indiana sky turned Dorothy Gale gray to see if they would show their thin ribbed underbellies. I learned early the important life-or-death difference between a tornado "watch" (the conditions are prime for a tornado in the area) and a tornado "warning" (get in the bathtub and grab your helmet because the house is going to blow away). Tornado warnings were serious business, especially if you're my mother's daughter. At the first sign of trouble, she gathered us into our small bathroom, giving us a breathless lesson about how small interior rooms are safest in a storm, but if you can't get to one, at least hunker down in the threshold of a doorway until the storm has passed.

Continuing our metaphor, we've arrived at a threshold of our own. You may not yet know if it's time to leave a particular room behind. But you're doing important work of naming where you are and what type of ending you may be facing, which are vital first steps when discerning where you're going. This is how we name the path we've traveled to get us here: pointing and calling, and asking questions to help us consider the rooms of our lives, including the ones where we belong, the ones we've left, and the ones we're not sure about yet. We're lighting a candle in the rooms of our lives, and the light grows stronger with each question.

Which rooms are still for me, and which rooms am I still for?

Which rooms am I questioning, and which ones might be questioning me?

Where do I sense caution flags?

Are they yellow or are they red?

What type of ending is this?

After many years of hosting conversations and writing about decision-making and discernment, I've learned that the best indicators of future decisions are the decisions we've already made. That means in order to move forward, we have to look back.

This may not be your favorite. I hope you'll hang with me.

For years I've had a regular practice of reflection, and it's been one of the most transformative practices I've engaged in. Paying attention to rooms I've entered and exited before and what was life-giving and life-draining in those situations is an excellent teacher for the future. But when we have a decision to make, our tendency is to look for a path ahead, not realizing that the only path available to us is the one we've already walked. When it comes to our lives, we're always only standing at the start.

Spanish poet Antonio Machado wrote a compelling poem that puts a finer point on this concept: "Caminante, no hay camino," translated as "Traveler, There Is No Road." The overarching message of the poem is that *the path is made by walking.*

Contemporary poet Lynn Ungar expounds on these lines in her poem called simply "The Path":

> *The path only unfolds behind us,*
> *our steps themselves laying down the road.*
> *You can look back and see the sign posts—*
> *the ones you followed and the ones you missed—*
> *but there are no markers for what lies ahead.*[1]

Our good work, then, is not to try to find the path before us but to name the path behind us, the one we've walked that's brought us to the sacred now. This is the second letter of our PRAY acronym—*Remember your path*—and it's what we'll unpack next.

Whether we're walking into new rooms, leaving old rooms, or growing within the rooms where we stay, reflection serves as a key spiritual practice. No matter their outcome, personal decisions we made in the past are often our best teachers. The ones that resulted in wins and losses. The good, the bad, even the indifferent—all of our past decisions have something to teach us. It applies to not only our individual pasts but also our collective one.

Looking back at my own path, I know the early rooms of faith I found myself in were formative. I met my friend Jesus at age seven, under the guidance and prayers of my quiet mother, inside the walls of the little white house on Gladstone Avenue in Columbus, Indiana. I was taught that God wanted to have a personal relationship with me, and the words we used to talk about God and faith were simple, relational, and individual.

When she wasn't double-checking that the stove was turned "Off, off, off, off," one of my favorite things to do with my mom was to sing from her hardbound green hymnal. We would spread it out between us, the book lopsided, lying half on her grown lap and half on my small one, open to "Just as I Am," "How Great Thou Art," or "What a Friend We Have in Jesus." We would pile ourselves sideways into that overstuffed recliner rocking chair in the corner, belt out the melody in unison because it was the only way we knew, and sing those hymns for what felt like hours. It was probably no more than a few minutes at a time, but the memory lives on, and my faith came easy, like playing Barbies on a Saturday morning.

In the months and years following my own profession of faith, talking to Jesus was the most natural thing in the world to me, so much so that one of my earliest school memories is sitting with a friend on the swings at L. Frances Smith Elementary School and telling her all about Jesus and heaven and didn't she want to pray to ask him to come live inside her heart like a tiny best friend? Why would anyone say no to that? I couldn't imagine. It's only been upon reflection that I vaguely remember she and her family attended a Methodist church in town. It did not occur to me that she might, in fact, already have faith in God. She might actually already know my tiny best friend. Maybe to her Jesus was a great big friend. I don't know. I never asked.

Receiving an expression of faith from your parents at an early age brings gifts and burdens we'll spend a lifetime unpacking. For me, I learned the unmatched comfort of a church potluck and how God the Father, God the Son, and God the Holy Spirit could show right up at the dessert table. I learned how to play the handbells and the words to all 129 verses of "Just as I Am." I learned and believed that God was, at the core, *good*, that God was for me, and could be trusted. I learned that if I had a question, I probably shouldn't ask it, because that would show there's stuff I don't know, and that seemed like a bad idea to let people in on. No one told me that, but somehow I picked it up.

There was a comfort and an at-home-ness to the low-churchy-ness of our Southern Indiana faith community, then later, another church in South Carolina. I'm grateful for the gifts of my spiritual upbringing and I'm still discovering the parts that were left out. One of the less emphasized and therefore underdeveloped aspects of my personal spiritual formation growing up in the particular evangelical churches we attended is that I learned our faith was primarily *personal*. And while this is of course true, I lacked a full understanding of the importance of community and the diversity of the global church. While I learned about the regular gathering of people, I missed the part about how the church is more than just *my* church and how God's people don't always look like me. Church is where my earliest narratives began to form about God and faith, community and responsibility, about what it means to stay, and what it means to walk away. This reflection, while incomplete, is one way of pointing and calling to my own path, specifically as it relates to my life with and experience of the Divine.

In late 2019, many of those underdeveloped aspects of my spiritual upbringing began to rise to the surface. By now our church was settled into the new building, our family had a solid routine with our community group, and we served together on a monthly basis, preparing the table for Communion and the sanctuary for worship. But after service on Sundays, John and I would trade stories of growing discomfort. We were compelled to stay and weren't at that time thinking about making a change. But we were becoming increasingly uncomfortable with some of the ways the church operated, and we weren't the only ones. Many of our friends at the church shared our discomfort, but John and I kept our most detailed conversations just between us. We asked ourselves many of The Ten Questions—not formally but regularly.

Did we choose this room? Yes.

What is good and beautiful here? So much.

Are there corners we're avoiding? Absolutely.

What is our role to effect change? We aren't sure.

We expressed to each other our shared frustration about who was missing in the room as well as who had already walked out the door. We held a real and painful tension between this community of people, whom we loved, and the larger system within which the community operated. We may not have named it a point-and-call practice at the time, but that's what we did each week for many months, working to name our discomfort and identify if the caution flags we sensed were merely yellow or blaring red.

Anytime we bring our awareness forward to what is true right now, we may wonder what to do with the information we gather. Where do we put our questions, our facts, our gut feelings, our nagging thoughts, and our newly realized realities? Even if the practice of pointing and calling reveals something you either hadn't named or hadn't noticed before, awareness doesn't automatically imply that there needs to be a change. In fact, sometimes awareness can bring great relief. Maybe you thought you had to leave the room for good, when really you only needed to have one difficult conversation, make a few small adjustments, or change the way you're showing up. Like wearing a coat inside the house, pointing and calling can help you realize you have the power to control the thermostat. Of course that's not always the case, but sometimes it is and we don't realize it until we point and call.

If pointing and calling uncovers a reality that all is not well or at least all may not be well for the road ahead, how do we know what to change, when to make a move, or how big a move to make? As with most things in this process, it depends. One of the things it depends on is what matters most to you. In part 2, we'll enter the hallway: a time to hold the tension of our decisions, to take a second and sometimes third look at what is holding us back, and to examine and evaluate our rooms and scripts as we discern if it's good to stay or if it's time to find a new way. But first, let's remember our path by exploring two simple guideposts that we may not even be aware have already been guiding our way.

The process of decision-making is one of my favorite things to talk about because it's a dynamic, deeply personal, and always changing landscape. But it's also one of the things that has given me the most trouble in my life. What decision should I make? How can I know for sure? What if I wreck it all up?

When we're unsure or hesitant about making a decision, our tendency might be to make lists, to ask our people, and to weigh the pros and cons. Of course all of these things can be helpful. But one of our greatest teachers is one we often ignore, possibly because it can be the hardest to hear: It's us. It's our very selves, our own desire, our intuition, and the movement of God in the midst of it all, who is, as philosopher and author Dallas Willard said, "the great being . . . who fills and overflows all space, including the atmosphere around our body."[2] At the most basic level, making decisions in a better way starts with understanding that we don't make decisions in a vacuum. There are too many factors at play that give color, texture, and nuance to every single decision we make, even the small ones. As much as we may think otherwise, it's impossible to approach decisions apart from who we are because our choices are born out of our character.

We'll practice looking back in order to uncover what we'll refer to broadly as personal guideposts, those markers along your life path that have already served as arrows for you along the way. They help you to know you're moving in a direction that's aligned with who you are today and how you are created to move through the world. Because this good work of discernment doesn't begin when you have a giant decision to make. As Irish philosopher and novelist Iris Murdoch said, "At crucial moments of choice most of the business of choosing is already over."[3] When it's time to make a decision, we tend to move on instinct. So how can we become the kind of people whose instincts are to move and choose with wisdom, generosity, courage, and love? One way to begin is by knowing and naming our personal guideposts, defined by our spiritual personality (or how we connect with God) and our personal core values (or what matters most to us). These are lived out through chosen behaviors and the unique expression of our personhood. Let's take a closer look at the first guidepost: spiritual personality.

In the eighth grade I was thrilled to be invited to go on a beach trip with a group of three other girls and one of their moms. These were girls I liked, and I was glad they wanted to be around me. But a week or so before the trip, one of them came up to me at school, saying she thought maybe I should rethink my decision to go to the beach with them after all. "You probably wouldn't have any fun," she said. "We're just looking out for you," she said. "It's for the best." How thoughtful.

But my brain wasn't fully developed and I didn't have the ability to read between the lines, so I pressed her, confused as to why she thought I wouldn't have fun. "I would have so much fun! I want to go! Wait, why can't I go? Am I being uninvited?"

She finally spit it out: "Well, we just won't want to sit in the hotel room and read our Bibles all day like you will."

Oh.

Face burning red, tears stinging in my eyes, I tried to assure her that's not what I would do, that's not what I would *want* to do. But the verdict was out and the ruling was final: I was too Jesus-y to have fun at the beach. It was out of their hands. This was my fault. And I was dismissed.

It was, as you can imagine, relationally devastating. I lost those friendships after that and all because of my faith. At least, that's the martyr-ish way my eighth-grade self framed it. Maybe I was just kind of a boring kid—who can say? What could I have done to convince them? Where did I go wrong? I wasn't a person who brought my Bible to school. I didn't wear corny Christian T-shirts. I listened to reasonably cool music like everyone else. But somehow they had sniffed out my deep devotion to God and they weren't interested. It would take me years to be proud of eighth-grade me, to be grateful for avoiding a worse heartbreak that would've surely come if I had gone with them and been excluded without a way of escape. And it would take even longer for grown-up me to have compassion for myself at that age, the girl who did adhere too rigidly to a standard I thought God had for me and probably, unknowingly, judged the kids around me for not living up. I have had to forgive myself for all the ways I thought I was better than everyone else. Oh, the depths of grace we all need.

The reality is, they didn't get it all wrong. I did love to read the Bible. Not at school, and I wouldn't have done it at the beach. But those kids picked up on a part of my spiritual personality that was true: *I loved to learn about God.* I thought deeply about matters of faith, and I was motivated to experience God and to learn more. I have my mother to thank for introducing me to Jesus, and the faith communities of my younger years for teaching me one way to walk with him. But as always is the case for any healthy faith, my understanding of what it means to walk with God continues to grow.

One of the most generative realizations about life with God over the past decade has been to understand that faith and spiritual expression don't look just one way. This is a vital revelation to have, especially when you're discerning if a particular room is a place for you to be.

In his book *Sacred Pathways*, Gary Thomas submits nine ways we connect with God, depending on our own personalities. He writes that we all will most likely resonate with at least one, if not several pathways, and they may change over time. This is not an exact science but one tool of potentially many to help us consider how we might most naturally connect with God. From the following nine spiritual pathways suggested in Thomas's book, see if there is one that resonates most with you.

> *Naturalists* love God through the natural world and feel closest to God outside in the midst of creation. Whether it's the mountains, forest, or ocean, being in nature awakens the naturalist to God's presence and beauty.
>
> *Sensates* connect with God through the experience of the senses: beautiful music, compelling art, or even through the simple light or smell of a warm candle.
>
> *Traditionalists* are drawn to ritual and symbol, embracing the

historic dimensions of their faith. They may enjoy God through habits like morning and evening prayer or liturgical practices with a faith community.

Ascetics connect with God through meditation, simplicity, or journaling. They are drawn to silence and solitude and tend to avoid what they might call the "trappings of religion and the noise of the outside world."

Activists are compelled by a greater vision for the world. Confronting corrupt systems, standing up for the marginalized, and fighting for justice and equity are ways they most deeply connect with the Divine.

Caregivers are drawn to other people and experience God most profoundly when loving others, even if it calls for significant sacrifice on their part. They love God best as they love others well.

Enthusiasts are compelled by worship, music, and mystery. They are energized to express their connection with God through joyful celebration.

Contemplatives may have a rich, inner life of prayer and are drawn to God through adoration. They "seek to love God with the purest, deepest, and brightest love imaginable."

Finally, *Intellectuals* love God through the mind and come alive when they have the space to think deeply about theology.[4]

This last one may have been eighth-grade me, trying on the rhythm of an Intellectual who connects with God through learning and through my mind. I'm not sure it's the pathway that comes most naturally for me, but it was the one modeled for me in the communities where my faith was formed. I thought the main way to connect with God was through my mind, and that idea was reinforced and rewarded. It wasn't wrong, but it was incomplete.

Learning about these various spiritual pathways is a helpful framework for considering how we best connect with God. I think Gary Thomas's language is informative, but that doesn't mean it's exhaustive. It also doesn't mean that we connect with God in one particular way to the exclusion of all others. He's simply given some language to ways people may connect with God, and that language makes it easier to discuss and explore. What if there are as many ways of connecting with and expressing love for God as there are humans?

The term "spiritual personality" is one I first heard from my friend and colleague Keas Keasler, who adapted Gary Thomas's work in *Sacred Pathways*, changing the language from "pathway" to "personality." Both images can be helpful, but I slightly prefer "personality," as it calls to mind something that is intrinsic rather than external.

No matter what you call it, chances are you've had a narrow or abbreviated idea of what it means to connect with the divine presence of God regardless of your faith tradition or spiritual background. If your tradition elevates quiet contemplation and thoughtful silence, but your personality is one that is naturally drawn toward and comes alive in animated conversation with the people around you, then it's possible you've grown to believe that you don't have a pathway to connect with God, because the one that was modeled for you doesn't make sense to you. Or if your faith tradition taught you that raised hands and closed eyes during emotional times of worship was the only, or at least the main, evidence of connection with God, but you're drawn to quieter spaces and smaller gatherings, then it's possible you've believed a narrative that you aren't a spiritual enough person. The scripts handed to you from your particular faith traditions are lines you can memorize but aren't your native language.

Some communities of faith elevate particular gifts or personality traits over others, labeling them (either overtly or indirectly) as more spiritual than other gifts or personality traits. But all nine pathways (and more) count—like casting vision, preparing a meal, taking a walk, throwing a party, collecting leaves, practicing photography, gathering with people. All of these are human expressions of personality, desire, and life. All of these can be ways of connecting with God. Your pathway of connection shapes your spiritual personality. And your spiritual personality informs your personal guideposts for making decisions.

The goal is not to have named and narrowed your spiritual personality once and for all. Instead, consider the following questions to help you know and name your own spiritual personality for now:

What pathways do I immediately resonate with? Without thinking too deeply about them, is there one or two that stands out among the rest?

What activities, environments, and people draw me to God, to Light, to the Divine? Looking back over your life, consider times when God seemed to be near. What were you doing and who were you with?

Likewise, which ones feel the least natural and most foreign to me? Perhaps several of these pathways seem deeply uninteresting, intimidating, or unnecessary. Rather than judging yourself for being turned off, or distrusting others who resonate with those pathways, let this instead be useful information. Knowing what doesn't resonate is just as important as naming what does.

Is there a particular pathway that might open me up to a new experience of God? Where do you sense curiosity or invitation? Do any of these descriptions cause you to want to learn more?

Beyond these nine named ways of connecting with God, what is missing? What would you add to the list? What would you remove? What seems incomplete? How would you rework or rename what's listed here?

Carry these questions with you as you go along your way, paying attention to activities, movements, moments of the day, and environments that wake you up to God's presence in your life. How you connect with God has already been part of your path. This is one guidepost that you've likely been following throughout your life; you simply may not have named it yet.

While your spiritual personality is all about how you connect with God, your personal core values are all about what matters most to you. This is our second guidepost.

Without a guidepost, we lose our way. As we make our way through the fog of indecision, of doubt, of not being sure of what to do next, we're like travelers who can't see the landmarks in the fog. "The temptation," writes Margaret Silf in her book *Inner Compass*, "is to try to resolve the problem by effort and activity, with the result that you go round in circles, and if you are on dangerous ground, you may well fall down a crevice or off a cliff."[5] So here is where we continue to put language to our own inner compass.

Dallas Willard often said that everyone receives spiritual formation just like everyone gets an education, and that has nothing to do with church or school.[6] We are always being formed and educated, but the question is how? Toward what? Is our formation generative or degenerative, restorative or malformed? Are we moving toward God or away from God? What kind of education are we getting? What kind of formation is happening at the spirit level?

A similar principle holds true for our personal core values. We all have them, but are they named? Do we know what they are? And are they the ones we want them to be? Personal core values help us to know and name who we already are and what matters most to us.

The dangers of not knowing or naming your personal core values are many. You may naturally think the danger would be living a life "less than" the one you could be living. But the opposite is also true. You could become highly successful in a life you never wanted. You might allow other people's agendas to determine your yes and your no. You'll be more prone to manipulation, coercion, and doubt. You could lose a sense of grounding, always looking around rather than looking within. You could find yourself saying yes to a lot of great opportunities that lead to someone else's stage and fulfill someone else's agenda. It's possible to become very successful in a life that doesn't fit you. It happens all the time. Untapped potential and misaligned success are just two sides of the same coin. You cannot be formed inside someone else's life. You have to live your own life. That's why it's imperative to identify what matters most to you. Because what matters most will always inform your next right thing.

Here's the most important thing to know: you already have personal core values just like you already have a spiritual personality just like you already have a rhythm of life. The work here, then, is to begin to invite those defining parts of yourself forward, to point to them and call to them and begin to give them shape and language.

Here are five questions to help you name your own personal core values, those guiding principles that probably have already informed all your decision-making even if you aren't aware of what they are. You may want to give yourself margin to carry these questions with you as you go along your days, answering them over time, paying attention to your initial first-thoughts as well as responses that may hold more nuance or need more time to unravel.

What bothers me? We are often bothered when something that deeply matters to us is violated, bypassed, ignored, or devalued. Follow the threads of frustration and you may arrive at a deeply held personal value.

When was the last time I felt most like myself? What were you doing? Who was present? Who was absent? When we are living fully as the people who we most deeply are, chances are our personal core values are in alignment with that activity, setting, or group.

What inspires emotion in me? Tears and laughter can serve as tiny messengers from the deepest part of who we are. If we welcome them without apology, they will do good work within us, serving as arrows in our lives. They have the capacity to send a most important message, a gift sent from our inner life to remind us of desire, importance, and value. Pay attention to them.

What do I want to be true about the world? Sometimes our values are aspirational, something we hope to be true about us or the world around us, about our way of moving through the world. It doesn't mean we always act in accordance with this value, but thinking about what we hope to be true can help us begin to put language on what we value most.

What words, images, stories, or moments inspire me? There is no wrong answer here. Simply make a list of words or phrases, movies or books, memories or conversations that have stayed with you over time. Don't worry if they seem unrelated or random. When your list is complete, see if you can identify common threads or themes.

Knowing your spiritual personality and your personal core values are two key elements that inform your personal guideposts. A guidepost isn't necessarily something external that you can point to; rather it's another way of giving language to desire. "Desire" is a word many of us don't know what to do with. It's a hot-potato kind of word, one we don't want to linger with too long lest we get into trouble. But desire is simply energy, a motivating force toward something we long for. Can we be misled by desire? Yes. But can we also be misled by avoiding, fearing, or bypassing desire? Also yes. Perhaps a helpful thing to remember about desire is this: knowing and naming what you want is not the same as forcing or demanding what you want.

Demanding a desire be met is a form of aggression.

Naming a desire you have is an honest confession.

Our desire is our desire whether we name it or not. We get into trouble when we have a desire and demand it be met, in our way and in our time. But knowing and naming our desire is a gift to ourselves and to those around us. It's a way of honoring our life, of acknowledging the ways God might be moving in and around us, of pointing at and calling to the center of our being, of who we are and who we are becoming. Our desire may be fulfilled or it may not. But admitting what we long for is something to not only name; it's also something to protect, as it flows from our inner life. King Solomon understood the importance of this center, writing in Proverbs 4:23: "Keep your heart with all vigilance, for from it flow the springs of life."

Don't do the difficult, deep work of trying to discern whether or not it's time to stay or go until you've done the equally deep but often less obvious work of knowing yourself. Or as Parker Palmer puts it in *Let Your Life Speak*: "Before I can tell my life what I intend to do with it, I must listen to my life telling me who I am."[7]

As I've developed a robust practice of listening to my own life over the years, I've named the spiritual pathways I most naturally walk as that of the Naturalist (connecting with God in nature), the Ascetic (connecting with God through silence and solitude), and also sometimes the Traditionalist (connecting with God through liturgy and symbol). This combination can be at odds with itself since the Ascetic is compelled toward God in simplicity while the Traditionalist in me longs for the comfort and rhythm of liturgy and ritual. Over the years, I've narrowed my personal core values down to three simple words: "connection," "creativity," and "solitude." Knowing and naming my guideposts has been illuminating in my process of discernment.

It's 2019, and as we continue to pay attention to some caution flags in our church, I'm also in the middle of one of the busiest seasons of my professional life so far. For four years I've been co-running an online membership site for writers alongside my two co-founders. What started as a side-hustle hobby that made some extra spending money has turned into a full-time job. *Oops! We accidentally started a business.* I say that in jest, but it's partly true. We always hoped it would become something that would help people, that would encourage writers to make progress and make a positive difference in the world. Of course now that it has, we have new questions to hold and more complicated problems to solve. We're planning to hire our first full-time employee, we have a small team of part-time contractors who have stretched to keep pace with our fast-moving startup, and we're putting on a live event that seems to require not only every ounce of my attention but also a skill set that does not come naturally to me.

Outside of my work with this membership site, I'm two years into hosting *The Next Right Thing* podcast, I've just released *The Next Right Thing* book, and I've finally completed two long years earning my master's degree in spiritual formation. My body is exhausted and is telling me through random and unpredictable stomach-related issues, rapid weight loss, and a constant low-grade hum of anxiety. Underneath the activity, the busy schedule, and the sometimes fulfilling but always pressure-filled days, I'm carrying a question about my work with the business that I haven't articulated yet: *Is the time approaching for me to leave this room?*

I know I won't be co-running this business forever. I know a time will come when either it will end, we will sell, the internet will stop existing, or one or more of us will exit. But the road between where I am now and where I imagine I will one day be seems impossible for now. This room is tangled up in contracts, shared ideas, intellectual property, and money. There is no door; there are only windows.

In a move necessary for the health of my body and soul, I plan to take several weeks off from everything toward the end of the summer. I use the word "plan" lightly. I plan, but I'm not thorough. I leave some things half done, fail to have important, clarifying conversations with some new team members and my business partners, and know there will probably be a ridiculous pile of decisions that need to be made when I return, not to mention some difficult conversations. At this point, I can't care. I just need a break.

The first four weeks provide a much-needed time of rest, but apparently this isn't enough. Because during the fifth and final week I quietly enter back into work without telling anyone, to try to get ahead on some things before the meetings start up again. But even just that one secret week back has my mind and body in knots again. Before reentering fully into my work, I plan one final getaway and leave my zip code for a weekend at one of my favorite retreat centers in North Carolina. I arrive before dinner, enter the front doors to check in, and am greeted by a woman with kind eyes and a warm hug. The urge to sob is instant. While I've learned to honor the presence of tears without apology, I also know I don't have the emotional capacity to deal with the vulnerability hangover that will inevitably come later if I surrender to sobbing on this woman I've just met. Instead, I welcome the release of a few respectable tears, but even with that I still feel like a toddler, my emotions out of control. She shows me to my upstairs room, and as soon as I close the door, I collapse on the bed and stare up at the ceiling. My self-imposed sabbatical is nearly over. What am I going to do now?

It's a big question, but I don't have the capacity for big answers. Instead, I do my next right thing. I unpack my bag, place my books on the side table, and make my way downstairs for dinner. While there, I greet my fellow retreatants and we make casual small talk about the food and the weather. When dinner is over, I take a walk around the grounds, notice how the sky is a deeper shade of blue, notice how I'm drawn to the shadows beneath the distant trees.

The irony is that I am co-running a business that requires me to be creative, but the success of the business means I don't have margin for solitude, which is a requirement of creativity (two of my personal core values). During the two days at the retreat center, I take lots of walks, cry more than half the time, and wrestle with the thought that perhaps this time away is a waste. But I also trust that God often works within us good things we can't see or understand, and that invisible work is weaving its way through me as I walk the trails, notice the leaves, and pick up rocks to take home. I am a Naturalist walking a simple path with God. Something working within me that weekend is a deep desire for a change of pace, a longing for greater margin, connection, and creativity. These things are named and realized in nature and in solitude. *Keep your heart with all diligence, for from it flow the springs of life.*

I leave the retreat center without clear steps for the when, the why, or the how but with newly realized personal guideposts: I know I need *connection* with God and others, *solitude* to cultivate my inner life, and space for *creativity* to feel like a person. I don't have an exit plan, a date of departure, or a five-step process for what to do next. But after a few days of remembering my path by paying attention to the last year or so of my life and naming what has been life-draining and life-giving, I recognize the toll my schedule is having on my body and soul. Through this pointing and calling, I become aware that something has to change, that this business I'm co-running is good work but isn't my best work, and that though I am ready to exit, it isn't yet time.

The day I return home from my personal retreat, my executive assistant tells me her time working for me has come to an end, so I spend the next few months hiring her replacement. Sometimes you're the one leaving, other times you're the one left. It doesn't have to mean anything or anyone is wrong, but it's simply part of the healthy, human rhythm of leaving rooms and finding new ones. For her, it's time, even though I'm not ready. Six months after this, the world would shut down due to the COVID-19 pandemic, further prolonging any plans to make a change in my business.

It would be a full three years before I was finally able to leave the room, exiting the business I helped to start and build. Those years included hiring a large team, running the company fully remotely, lots of conflict management, loads of patience with myself and others, and a constant reminder that the work we were doing in the interim was good and important, even as I carried the reality that I wouldn't be here forever. Sometimes the decision to leave leads to quick movement and instant change. Often, though, leaving well actually starts with a choice to stay for now so that you can leave when the time is right. This may be years in the making, requiring patience, persistence, and a lot of grace.

Of the many things decision-making often requires of us, our creative imagination is most certainly one of them. If we don't give ourselves a bit of time and space to consider possibilities, to sit with potential, to let ideas and scenarios play out for a while, then our imagination will just do its knee-jerk thing. We'll make our decisions not based on our gifting, our values, or what matters most; we'll just make them to avoid pain, to avoid discomfort, to avoid disappointing others, or sometimes just to get the decision out of the way.

I once heard the executive dean of Portland Seminary MaryKate Morse ask an important question: "What embodies you with God and what gets you back to yourself?"[8] As you look for clues to your path forward, looking back to remember your path behind you may at first feel counterintuitive. As you continue to discern your next right thing as it relates to the rooms of your life, knowing and naming the path behind you will offer clarity about the path ahead as you name what embodies you with God (your spiritual personality) and what gets you back to yourself (your personal core values). Once you begin to put more language on your own inner compass, you may discern an invitation to change your mind.

Practice Changing
Your Mind

We have an addiction to the idea that learning can
happen without pain.

—PÁDRAIG Ó TUAMA, *IN THE SHELTER*

Oftentimes an ending is what happens when a mind is changed, either yours or someone else's. Because you're reading this book, chances are good either you're wondering if you should change your mind, you've already changed your mind about something, or someone has changed their mind about you.

If you wanted to, you could spend your whole life studying the science behind how (and why) people change their minds. I haven't done that kind of study, but I have been paying attention to moments along the way when I thought something and then when things changed. In a book of discernment about whether or not it's time to stay or go, it's vital to have a conversation about one of the biggest obstacles to answering the question: a hesitation to change your mind. A way to ease us into the conversation could be to point out the ordinary liturgy of changing our minds that we've been engaged in through our whole lives. (Again, the path is behind us.)

Growing up in the Midwest, the extent of my exposure to seafood was either fish sticks from a box or my dad's Filet-O-Fish sandwiches from McDonald's. (To this day, if you go to McDonald's with Dad, he will order the fish sandwich.) I didn't regularly eat seafood until I met John. It was a whole new food group to me. I learned I liked salmon and mahi-mahi but don't care for tuna or trout.

I used to write in secret, never wanting anyone to read my words. Now I'm an author and I make my living by sharing the words I write. Growing up, we laughed at the bell-bottoms and pointy collars those shaggy-haired kids wore on *The Brady Bunch*, but by college, my favorite pants were my wide-leg, flare corduroys, a style I still love to this day. In elementary school, I was the quietest one in class, and now I talk for a living. In the Midwest, I grew up saying "you guys" when referring to a group of people, but now I can't go a day without unironically saying "y'all." We rolled our eyes at country music when I was a kid, but by college I had George Strait's "Love Without End, Amen" playing on a loop. I thought my love of language and posture for translation would always look like sign language interpreting, but as it turns out, it also looks like finding ways to re-language faith and transformation through writing and spiritual direction. I changed my mind, over and over again.

We've been changing our palate, our likes, our preferences, and our obsessions for our whole lives. When our taste buds change, we say they've "matured." When our fashion sense changes, we say it's "evolved." But food and fashion are low-stakes subjects. Those are rooms we generally leave and enter with a spirit of curiosity, a willingness to try something out, knowing that the door will open easily if we want to walk through it again. But in those areas where the stakes are higher, like our vocation, our politics, our relationships, or our religion, change is more threatening. Those rooms have heavier furniture, stronger relational bonds, and deeper pockets. Leaving those rooms doesn't just require a change of taste but also a change of mind and, in some cases, a change of being.

"That smoke is thick. Are you sure we can go this way?"

It's morning and the sky behind us is blue, but the sun in front is just an idea, hidden by a thick pink and gray smoke in the east.

"I'm just following the traffic."

John cranes his neck forward over the steering wheel, the way we do when we think it will help us see what's coming up ahead, a posture we've grown accustomed to over the last year.

It's late January 2012 and we're in Florida for a long weekend. His dad died of lung cancer six months earlier, and we've lived through a deep season of grief, questions, and change. Today we're holding our own questions about the future during this weekend away in Florida, where we've come to do some thinking, some resting, and some planning. We come up with answers and are as honest as we're able to be, but deep down we wonder what's next. This simple question leaves an existential echo in our souls.

John turns the rental car into the line of traffic as we move closer to the source of the billowing smoke. I can see it now, just beyond the shoulder. We're one in a long line of cars crawling forward, parallel to the pine forest that lines the highway. And that's when we see that all the trees are on fire.

"I'm rolling down my window," I say. I'm tentative, it's counterintuitive, but I'm compelled to take a photo with my phone, and I don't want the window glass to obscure the view. It's especially cold this morning for Florida, and I expect the chill to fill the car, but I'm shocked by the wall of intense heat that hits my face when the window comes down, heat that instantly enlarges my pores.

There's a wall of fire, but there's no emergency here. Fire experts line the highway and stand by while the brush burns up. I learn later it's what they call a prescribed, or controlled, burn. It looks dramatic, but it's under control—planned and prepared for. This fire has boundary lines, with keepers who watch and wait and guard the beginning and ending—a predictable narrative arc.

Controlled burns are set for good purpose. We can learn the most about controlled burns from Indigenous peoples, who have been practicing the ancient art of deliberate burns in North America and around the world for millennia.[1] They restore ecosystem health and prepare an area for new vegetation, which in turn helps to support various habitats for different species. Controlled burns can also reduce the amount of overgrowth in an area in order to minimize the risk of, for example, a small campfire causing an actual forest fire. They intentionally set low-intensity fire in order to keep an unintentional fire from burning out of control. Still, these intentional fires are hot.

I've never been this close to a fire of this scope and size, one where I can actually feel the heat. But I've witnessed the burning. About six months after moving to Iowa in the late 1980s, the house across the street from ours caught on fire. They said it started in the sauna. I remember that word because I didn't know what a sauna was. To this day, when I hear the word "sauna" I think of that house fire on our quiet Iowa street during the winter of fifth grade. I picture the dad of the family, whose name I didn't know, sitting in a white towel in a wood-lined room, heat pouring out of the walls. I think of him leaving the sauna and going to bed but forgetting to turn the knobs to OFF, if that's even how saunas work. So the sauna stayed on and somehow started a fire and everything changed for them. I think of waking in the middle of the night to the sound of breaking glass, of staring out the window of my parents' bedroom, the whole street blinking red from emergency lights. Mostly, I think of the smell, our most potent memory maker, and that's what I remember. If you've ever had a house fire or been near one, you know what I mean.

This isn't the familiar, nostalgic smell of an October bonfire or the gentle smoke after a burned-out candle. What burned in that house was not mere wood or wax. What burned were countertops, blankets, sofas, metal, plastic, pictures, and memories. The rancid, ashy smell of loss lingered on our street for months.

No one was hurt in that fire, which makes this an easier story to tell. Some of the family got out through various windows, but the neighborhood rumor was that at least one person walked out through the front door, opened it wide, inviting all that clean oxygen in, feeding the fire a feast. The thing that brought freedom for the trapped sent the whole place up even faster.

The memory of that night has lingered for decades. I say it burned down, but that's not an accurate picture of what happened. It didn't burn all the way to the ground; it burned *out from the inside.*

The next day and for months after, even though that Iowa house was ruined, the structure still stood, shutters framing lifeless windows, a roofline intact. It was just a building, a still yard with overgrown grass. It was empty, but if you didn't look too close, it appeared normal-ish. It loomed present but also absent. At night when I looked out across our lawn and tried to peer into the darkness, the house blended into the heavy shadows between the neighboring houses. If I didn't know it was there, I wouldn't have known it was there. Sometimes fire burns the insides but leaves the outside alone.

Changing our mind can feel like being in a burning house and finally opening the front door, escaping into fresh air. And it's such a relief, until you realize the very thing that saved you sent the room you left straight up in flames. Just because something burns doesn't mean you did the wrong thing by opening the door. At the same time, not all fires are created equal, and just because you feel the flame doesn't mean something has gone terribly wrong or even that you're in danger.

Fire is always hot, and flames have no respect for our intention; they just set the path to burn. It's dangerous if it catches you by surprise, you don't know what you're doing, or you don't have a way out. An accidental fire has great potential for trauma and lasting pain. What if changing our minds could be less like a house fire and more like a prescribed burn: healing and expected?

When it comes to ideologies and long-held ideals, author Sharon

McMahon (known online as America's Government Teacher) says, "Anyone who changes their mind based on new and better information is criticized and denounced. So it disincentivizes people from using critical thought when in reality the ethical thing is to change your mind based on new and better information."[2] When we are identifying the rooms where we live and work and worship, and we begin to discern some of them are still for us and others may not be for us anymore, the stakes are high. Even more so when a room isn't for us anymore because of who it has left out, kicked out, or excluded. We may be defensive against any new or better information. We may fear what considering that new information will require of us. This is something that may keep us in rooms way past time.

In the fall of 2015, back when our church still met in the warehouse sanctuary, the word around our small community was that an old friend was coming to town to visit and she was bringing her girlfriend. She was a former student of John's, one we had watched grow up through her early teen years and into college, a beloved babysitter whose photo we still had tacked up on our hallway bulletin board. We mostly lost touch when she moved away. I did not know she was gay. I was curious to see her again, looking forward to catching up if our paths crossed. It happened sooner than I expected when she and her girlfriend decided to visit our church. At this point we had only been part of this church for about two years and we were still finding our place there. I was surprised at their willingness, their openness, to come sit among us. They assumed we would be welcoming, at least. They assumed we would be neutral, I guess. So they visited a few times, and they were the only openly gay couple at our church.

A few years before that, I had read a book about the conversation around sexuality and spirituality by an author who desperately wanted to build bridges between his gay friends and the Christian faith he held on to. At the time, I wasn't close with any member of the LGBTQ+ community, at least none I knew of. But I had a lot of questions and angst around the topic. I knew what I'd been told all of my life growing up in our particular evangelical churches. I was familiar with their interpretation of the verses in the Bible that seemed to speak about homosexuality. But my questions were deep and wide, like a fountain flowing. Most things fit in my faith at the time, and the things that didn't fit, I felt peace to ignore (at least that's what I told myself). This was one of the things that did not fit. There was within me a growing discomfort, and I did not experience peace in ignoring it.

I remember exactly two things from that book. First, I was hyper-focused on a single question: I wanted to know the author's "stance." I became low-key obsessed trying to figure it out. This was not the point of the book, as it turns out. And second, I remember that after I read it, I became comfortable with my questions even though I didn't have answers. I was content with loving people without having to defend or explain who they loved in return. I'm not saying that was a good place to be or a sufficient place to stop. But I convinced myself it was enough for now. We tend to worship the expert, the knower of answers, the explainer of things. We don't like to be the learners or the holders of questions. We also don't like to be wrong.

That was 2013. Two years later, it all went well at first when our friends visited our church. And by "well," I mean there were no confrontations and no sermons about homosexuality. This was a church full of people who loved God as they understood God, who were creative and imaginative and thoughtful. This was a church we arrived at for the first time one year after our trip to Florida, where we saw the controlled burn, exhausted after twelve years in ministry. It's the church that became for us, for a time, a place of healing, a place of community, a place of shared joy, broken bread, and awakened creativity. This was the church where our kids would spend most of their elementary and middle school years and a place we loved and where we called home.

All of that was fully true. What was also fully true was that I was preemptively anxious and embarrassed for what I knew would eventually happen to this young gay couple if they stayed around long enough.

Almost immediately after I learned this couple was planning to visit our church, I had an experience that was so regular, so clear and normal, that I hesitate to call it an experience. It was more like a thought, like *my* thought except I knew it didn't come from me. If I've ever known anything for sure, I know this: the Spirit of the living, loving God has told me directly to do very few things in my life. But one thing God said to me, that I am as clear about as my own name, was, *When they walk out in the middle of the service, you follow them.* I wasn't even at church when I had this thought. Nothing had happened; no one was around. But it was not a suggestion or an idea. It was an action I was to take, no matter what. That's all I knew for sure.

There are some things that are just good advice. Keep your car's fuel tank a quarter full to lessen your chances of running out of gas. Wear sunscreen so you don't get a sunburn. Don't put your hand on a hot stove. These are common sense but also preventative. *Do these things so something bad doesn't happen.* But then what if the bad thing happens? When you run out of gas, call AAA. When you get a sunburn, use aloe. When you touch a hot stove, call 911 depending on how bad the burn is. *When this happens, then take this action.* That's what this statement was for me. It was a sure thing, not just in case.

I was nervous, because it seemed like the kind of thought that was a preparation for something inevitable rather than an optional action if the day ever came. Weeks went by. Maybe months? I'm not sure. And then, the day came.

John is teaching the children downstairs this morning, so I'm sitting alone near the back row of chairs. She and her partner arrive and sit next to me, another mutual friend on their other side. The man preaching today isn't one of the pastors but is a guest teacher who preaches from time to time. He's a respected voice in our church, holds a privileged position in our community. Near the end of his sermon, I feel her body stiffen beside me as he casually points out the "sin of homosexuality" while talking about the relevancy of scripture, wielding the Bible like a blunt instrument. And I realize in this moment that this would always be where the conversation starts and ends. *Sin* would always have the first and last word when it comes to the LGBTQ+ community in this church. Not Jesus, not dignity, not compassion or curiosity or hope. I hear it through her ears, his tone dismissive and othering. His words seem to be received by the congregation as business as usual, nothing to see here, what time is lunch? But for this friend, those words usher her and her partner out of our sanctuary for good.

How swiftly she gathers her things, grabs her sunglasses, leans down for her purse. How polite they both are to wait until a natural transition in the service before they get up. How quiet their footsteps are on the way to the door. At the front of the sanctuary, the elements are laid for Communion. At the back, these two young women leave the church without a word.

It's the scene I've imagined in my mind a hundred times before now, rehearsed in my imagination.

They're walking out.

The hand is on the stove.

Now.

Go.

When I get to the parking lot, they're walking away fast. I call my friend's name, and they both turn. And here is where I realize my first mistake. Because for all this time, I knew exactly what I would *do: When they walk out, you follow them.* And here it was, like a future I had already lived, like a prophecy come true. I was living it out and doing the thing. But I had never bothered to think, to ask, to consider what I would *say*. And so when I get there, standing in front of them, pain on their faces, I don't know how to be or what to do next. I have zero words to say. I don't know what I think; I haven't sorted out the theology; I don't have my questions answered.

All I know is something isn't right. All I know is something hasn't been right for a long time. All I know is I couldn't let them leave that room without following them out. With a lack of something to say, I hug my friend, and she lets me. I mutter a weak apology without yet knowing the depths of why. I cry a little and she cries more. She's angry and so am I, but I don't know how to show it, not yet. Her partner is silent, standing to my left, her patience palpable, like she knows something I don't know, like she has compassion for something I can't see. I hug them both, wish I could do more, but my ill-equipped imagination doesn't have room to think what that could be.

Years later, I'll recount this moment to a counselor and she'll ask, "What do you see in that moment? What emerges when you go back there in your mind?" At the time of the question, all I see is a dark unknowing mystery. I feel heartbroken and sad. I feel like I'm forgetting something, like I have reverse amnesia for a life I haven't yet lived.

We part ways there in the parking lot after I say nothing important, my inadequate presence hovering at the doors of the church. And then comes this one moment I will question for years to come. I wanted to love them and to show them I loved them. I was working hard to reconcile the theology I thought I knew with the humans in front of me. It wasn't adding up, but I didn't have the language or the courage to put words to that. As they walk to their car, I turn and walk back into the sanctuary. And I will stay at this church for five more years. Until the day comes when I can't stay there any longer.

When they walked out of the doors of my church, my friend Jesus told me to follow them. It was clear as the actual day. It was not an option to ignore that invitation. And so I went. I'm grateful for at least that much movement. Following them out was the least good thing. There was so much more. Our church was still a place we loved and were committed to. But that day in the parking lot, I received new and better information, human information, the kind you can only get through proximity. But I didn't know what to do with it. Or I did, and I didn't want to do it. I walked out of the room for a minute, but the hallway I found myself in was filled with too many questions and not enough answers. And so I chose what felt like certainty over what I anticipated to be a free fall of curiosity and disconnection and loss.

Sometimes our minds change in an instant, and other times it takes years and years to turn around, to see what we've been missing. By the time I stood in that parking lot, my posture was already on a path to softening, but the change was slow. It took me too long to empathize with the hurt and pain Christians have inflicted, to understand my role in that hurt because of my lack of willingness to dialogue, to take a second and third look, to listen and learn and pay attention. It took me too long to recognize that this group of humans who may feel unsafe in the world on a daily basis, always aware of their surroundings to assess if they belong, should at the very least be able to drop their guard inside the walls of a church, should feel the safest among people who know and love God. But it was not to be.

Still, this moment in the parking lot did important work inside me. It made it so I couldn't ignore the question any longer. I couldn't avoid conflict just to keep the peace that was really no peace at all. Because now I was brought near. Now this wasn't a distant issue to consider or an impersonal problem to solve; this was people I respected and cared about. When it comes to changing our minds, proximity is a most compelling companion: proximity to people, to their pain, and to the God who loves us all.

We don't always know which kind of fire we're in the middle of. The forest next to the highway in Florida burned up the brush on the ground, clearing the way for new growth, leaving the trees tall and strong. The house across the street burned down on the inside, shocking the inhabitants, taking all the good within, leaving an empty structure without life. That day in the parking lot, a white-hot spark of conviction continued to burn a flame, tiny but strong. Initially it may not be clear what kind of fire is burning in a particular room. All we know is we feel the heat of the kindling flames. They are all real fires: one was healing, the other tragic, the third a combination of both. We don't always know what kind of fire we've got, but for beauty to come from ashes, something has to burn.

There's a word people use in circles of faith, another way of languaging the ordinary liturgy of changing your mind. The word is "repentance."

Brian McLaren points out that this word means to "re-pent, to be pensive again. To re-think something. Life is a lifelong process of re-thinking."[3] I'll add to that and say life is a lifelong process of re-thinking, re-feeling, re-experiencing, re-deciding, re-moving, re-believing, re-seeing, re-newing. And maybe even re-olding—finding new ways to express and reconcile old things. "Repentance" is a word that may conjure up all kinds of images, depending on your faith (or lack of faith) context. In Christian theology, "repent" comes from the Greek transliteration *metanoia* and means both to change one's mind and to experience a transformative change of heart. This is not just a cognitive change. It implies a turning away but also a turning toward. It's no good to practice change just for the sake of it. But as we do our next right thing, as we continue to pay attention to love, as we turn, again and again, toward God, change is often an outcome. And we need not be so afraid of it.

This is deep and difficult work, and it's easy to opt out. Systems are strong and make it even harder for us to do the kinds of critical thinking and spiritual discerning that truly changing our mind often requires. There's a unique pain that comes from realizing it's time to move on from a group, idea, belief, or vocation that was once exactly right for you, or at least seemed exactly right. Maybe a decision was difficult, and you prayed and discussed and discerned that it was the "next right thing," yet because of time, growth, circumstance, or new information, you then realize it's time to make a change. What do you do when what was once your next right thing is no longer right for you? Did you hear wrong? Was your intuition off? Or is it something simpler and less threatening than that? We need to embrace changing our minds as an ordinary liturgy.

Today you may be walking around empty. And if no one looks too close, you may present okay, like the house in my neighborhood that burned only on the inside. But the truth is, a refining fire has swept through your life and you're still trying to figure out if this fire rendered a total loss or if anything is salvageable. You're still trying to figure out if this fire was an accident or if it was a controlled burn.

If you sense an invitation to pivot, to be the learner, the student, or the intern in any area of your life, it might be a good time to point and call. You might feel like you're walking into a dark room without a map, but maybe you don't need a map. Perhaps you only need some guideposts and a guide. The path is behind you, so recall your guideposts by reorienting yourself to your spiritual personality and personal core values. And remember your guide; the gift of God to the people of God is the with-ness of God who has not left us alone.

We've explored the universally appreciated elements of a good story that will result in a satisfying ending and one of them is transformation.

When Jerry Seinfeld decided to end his TV series in 1998 at the height of its popularity, the finale received mostly terrible feedback at the time. *USA Today* gave the final episode 1.5 stars out of 4, referring to it as the "dismal, dying moments of the final *Seinfeld*."

The critic went on to say: "I loved *Seinfeld* in the beginning, but over the years its infamous 'no hugs, no lessons' rule has worn thin.

Yes, it made the show avoid the facile sentimentality of other sit-coms, where people had an epiphany every week. But its refusal to have its characters learn and grow is just as artificial. In real life, our friends change."⁴

Jerry, George, Kramer, and Elaine were funny to watch. They said things you weren't allowed to say out loud, human and ridicu-lous things. But they weren't necessarily well-rounded people, and they were never meant to be. They were critical, petty, judgey, self-righteous, and they lacked empathy. We are all of those things too, but we aren't only those things. And the part that the reviewer picked up on is that these people never transformed. From begin-ning to end, they never changed. While that may seem like a com-pliment in a yearbook signing, and even works for a time in a sitcom, it's a terrifying thought to imagine always staying the same. In general, it doesn't make for a compelling story, and it's not the stuff of a compelling life.

When you're in the midst of beginning to change your mind about a script or a room, some point-and-call questions that could be helpful to ask are: What kind of fire is this anyway? Is God standing by, ever the expert, bearing witness to the refining, making space for new, good growth in this planned, controlled burn? Or is this a fire that has caught God by surprise? Is this a fire of destruction, taking the waste and the wellness alike? Sometimes our questions don't re-flect facts, reason, logic, or good theology. Sometimes our questions reveal our lack of faith, our fear, or our confusion. Ask them anyway. God has what it takes to sort it out.

If you sense a stirring, a whisper, a discontent within you that doesn't make sense but also seems right, please pay attention.

Sometimes when you change your mind, the growth is small and the burn is slow. It can be one you have to burrow and bury to hold safe while the growth takes root. Other times it's a change you wish you could share, but you can't because of NDAs, confidentialities, promises made, or secrets to keep. Your ability to understand it may be limited and your freedom to share it might be too. But being a person who enters into the ordinary liturgy of change is one who is growing. I've fiddled with the language and have tried on a few phrases. "Growing up" doesn't feel quite right because not all growth is "up." Some things grow down, like the roots of a tree, the rushing river water, the expression of divinity through the Christ child. "Growing away from"? That implies a running away, or a distancing from. And sometimes that's it, but not always. "Growing out of"? That implies I was a thing but now I'm a completely other thing. I've settled (imperfectly) on "growing into." We are always growing into ourselves, growing into our identity, growing into God.

Is there an area in your life where you've been holding on?

Is your jaw clenched against the possibility of change?

Does your stomach lurch when you imagine the amount of deep work it will take to begin to make a move in a different direction than the one you were handed, were taught, or worked so hard to get only to discover it wasn't what you thought it would be? Are you no longer who you once were?

You don't have to make all the moves right now. First, point and call. Name the rooms you're in and the ways they may no longer fit. Notice the yellow flags and consider if they're simply yellow or if they're turning red. Name the spaces in that room that you're drawn to and the corners you'd rather avoid. Name what happens in your body when you consider making a change and when you consider staying the same. Then, remember your path. Bring to mind the ways you connect with God and how that expression of connection is lived out through your personal core values. As you consider areas of your life where you are being invited to reconsider, reevaluate, or take a second look, here are some questions to carry along the way:

What is worth protecting?

What do I need to unlearn?

Who has already left this room?

Who is entering now?

What am I growing into?

Where am I regularly practicing an ordinary liturgy of change?

Where am I hesitant to embrace the work that change requires?

To practice changing our minds as an ordinary liturgy in daily life makes it so that when the large decisions show up that require a large-scale change of mind or heart, we already have some muscle memory to allow deep, transformative work to happen within us.

Part 2

ON PAUSING:

Discernment
in Hallways

We've spent time looking around at the rooms of our lives and the scripts that come with them, naming the ones we're questioning or the ones that are questioning us. We've entered into a practice of pointing and calling, acknowledging what is true without judgment or commentary. We've admitted that sometimes what prevents us from leaving or making a shift is a deeply held negative narrative attached to quitting or ending something we started. We're also learning to make peace with changing our minds.

We're taking deep breaths and practicing patience; we're learning how to know what we want and call it good; we're reconnecting with God again in a way that resonates with our own personalities. We're naming what matters to us in the form of our own personal core values. And all these tools we'll bring into our metaphorical hallway to help us discern what to do next. We'll do it together. We'll take it slow.

Is it time to make a shift or a change?

Is it time to settle all the way in right where I am?

Is my time in this room coming to a close, whether by choice or by force?

For the purpose of our continued conversation, here's what we're talking about when we say "hallway." A hallway is a place of permission. It's a space where you're allowed, compelled even, to ask your questions, perhaps the kinds of questions that your rooms haven't allowed. It's a space to try on possibilities and to reimagine what could be.

The hallway may be the space between two rooms, the place where you enter after you've already decided to leave. But it could also be a pause, a space where you enter just for a time, to clear your head, to take a beat, to weigh your options, to remember who you are. When your time in the hallway is past, you may reenter the room you just left and discover it's exactly right for you. Or at least right for now. Or the time in the hallway may be just what you need to get perspective and clarity on an inevitable ending.

The hallway is not only a waiting room, although it could be that. It's a waiting room, a bridge, and a deep breath. Sometimes it's a wilderness. Other times, a respite. The goal isn't necessarily to leave every hallway we find ourselves in, to find all the right rooms, to close and lock the doors, to paint the walls the colors that suit us, and to sit down forever.

We may stay in certain hallways for decades. Sometimes the hallway is the best we can do. Sometimes the hallway becomes a room all its own. And we gather with the misfits and the I-don't-know-yets, and all those who are leaving rooms but don't yet know where to go.

So while a hallway may be right for now, what I don't want to do is hang back in the hallway when I know it's time to walk into a room. What I don't want to do is stay in a room to avoid a hallway. What I don't want to do is linger too long on either side of the threshold in fear.

This hallway can be what you need it to be. If you're deeply attached and drawn to a room but need a space to rethink it, here is where you'll discover some good questions to ask, important movements to consider, and new language for old concepts that may be holding you back.

We'll have four conversations in this hallway: the importance of naming the arrows that come before answers, the difference between peace and avoidance, the distinction of readiness and timeliness, and the lack of closure in most of our endings. Here is where we will explore various movements that will cultivate the discernment that leads to clarity. By the end of this section, I hope these discernment practices will help you navigate a room you've already left, know if a change is needed and what kind of change that is, or discern if the room where you are is a good place for you to stay.

Welcome to the hallway.

Arrows and Answers

*We learn through pain that some of the things we
thought were castles turn out to be prisons, and we
desperately want out, but even though we built them,
we can't find the door. Yet maybe if you ask God for
help in knowing which direction to face, you'll have a
moment of intuition. Maybe you'll see at least one next
right step you can take.*

—ANNE LAMOTT, *HELP, THANKS, WOW*

Should I stay or should I go? (I hope for both of our sakes that
the 1982 hit by The Clash is not officially and forever lodged
in our minds as the theme song to our entire extended con-
versation. In your mercy, Lord, hear our prayer.) After nearly six
years of hosting a podcast all about decision-making and writing a
book on the same topic, I've been in countless conversations that
circle around this central question.

In my experience, this may be the right question. But it's also a difficult one to hold. First, it implies a binary, as if there are only two options. This is rarely the case. Second, it gives the impression that this is a onetime decision: stay or go, this or that, yes or no, forever. In reality, most of our decisions come slowly, are a series of deciding to stay today and again tomorrow. Not once and for all, but once for now and twice for later. The temptation is always to take the most efficient path and the one of least resistance. And so we look for ultimate answers to some of our most pressing life questions. But what we get instead are silent, nuanced, and hidden arrows to just one next right thing—no more and no less. This concept of arrows and answers, first introduced in my book *The Next Right Thing*, continues to stir up questions and conversation among readers and listeners.

An answer is what we realize or choose at the moment of decision. This is what we think we want, what we've been conditioned to look for. We know how to define a decision; it's obvious when we've made one and equally obvious when we've procrastinated or put it off. It can be embarrassing at best to hold a decision for too long without movement, dangerous at worst to do the same. We imagine ourselves making a clearheaded onetime call, an admirable leader without bias or emotion, questions or regret. What we often get instead of an answer is a sleepless night, circular reasoning, an overplayed scenario, and a head full of doubt. Eventually, we'll make a decision. Or we'll not make it and that becomes a decision all by itself. A decision cannot be avoided. But the thing we *can* avoid is the thing we need most but aren't naturally taught: discernment. This is the vital process that precedes a decision.

Of course decision-making and discernment are connected, but it's possible to rush or bypass the discernment process in order to get to the relief of a final decision. When we do this, we miss out on the formation opportunities to know God, to know ourselves, and to depend on our community.

The process of discernment is deeply inefficient. It takes time, self-awareness, patience, and nuance. A decision is much more attractive. It's clear, active, and final (at least it gives that impression). I would much rather have a decision to make than a move to discern. But when it comes to influencing change within or leaving meaningful, identity-forming rooms, we're rarely confronted with a simple, binary decision.

In a conversation with Enneagram coach and teacher Suzanne Stabile about her own experience of growing in discernment and self-awareness, she shared how she's become aware of her own tendency to jump in and offer help to everyone around her whether they're asking for her help or not. Now before she offers to help someone, she asks herself three questions:

1. What am I expecting in return? (reveals her motivation)

2. Does this person want my help? (opens her awareness to the lived-experience of others)

3. What is mine to do? (reminds her of assignment, vocation, call)

Her final action is the answer, or the decision: to help or not to help. But her three questions leading up to the action are arrows, part of her discernment process that allows her to reach her decision.[1]

My hope for the work we're doing here together is to build a foundation for your ongoing discernment process as you move to the healthy, human rhythm of leaving rooms and finding new ones, living your way into your next right thing. By the end of our time together, you may or may not have made a final decision about whether to stay put or move on. But my sincere hope is that you will have at least identified some clear arrows to follow along the way.

When it comes to the word and concept of "discernment," several key ideas and people may come to mind. While often used in religious settings, the process of discernment is useful more broadly for personal growth, for business decisions, for questions around relationships, and more. We'll circle back around to the broad usage because that's where I want to spend the majority of our time. But I think it will be helpful to start with how people may have first encountered the concept of discernment: in faith-based spaces.

In religious circles, "discernment" is often the word used when talking about making decisions in the presence of God and determining where the Spirit of God is moving. A more formal approach to discernment is derived from rules set down in the Spiritual Exercises by Saint Ignatius of Loyola, Spanish theologian and mystic, founder of the Society of Jesus (Jesuits), and from whom Ignatian spirituality gets its name. The Spiritual Exercises are a collection of meditations, prayers, and practices he developed to help people deepen their life with God. Ignatian spirituality also recognizes the need for accompaniment in the process of discernment, whether that is direction for a particular life decision or a companion to help discern the presence and movement of God in your life. This type of accompaniment may also be called "spiritual direction," a practice that has been transformative in my own life, as someone who has received spiritual direction as well as through serving as a companion, or spiritual director, for others. The work of a spiritual director is to create prayerful space on behalf of another. It's a countercultural practice of co-listening for anyone who wants to deepen their awareness of and relationship with God. It allows space for curiosity, discovery, and held silence. In spiritual direction, while one person listens to another without an agenda, both people submit to the movement of God.

One communal approach to discernment and decision-making comes from the Religious Society of Friends (the Quaker tradition), called a clearness committee. Rather than one-to-one accompaniment, a clearness committee consists of a small group of people who gather to help a person discern how the Spirit might be moving in their life. The traditional purpose of a clearness committee was to discern the suitability of marriage under the care of a Friends meeting or suitability for membership within a Friends meeting.[2] But non-Quakers have also benefited from the companionship of a clearness committee, and some associated with Quakers have participated in this small group structure for personal discernment as well. This process cannot be rushed, and the Friends will patiently wait in silence with prayer and questions on behalf of the focus person seeking discernment and direction from God.

There are many wonderful books written on discernment from specific points of view, and I've borrowed concepts from many of them and practiced them in my own life. But here is a book for you, no matter your faith background or current reality, no matter the corporate structure of your workplace, no matter the hierarchies or authorities of your family system. Rather than wrap the discernment process around one particular modality, I'm intentionally keeping things broad, working to keep language accessible, and finding simple tools to offer that are borrowed from many streams of wisdom and can apply to many different types of decisions you might be carrying.

Discernment is both a gift and a practice. For some, discernment is a character trait they are naturally prone to, having a sharp instinct or intuition about things, possessing uncanny judgment. Like those who are gifted at teaching or painting, a keen discernment might be a way you naturally see and relate to the world. But it's still something you can also cultivate and hone. It doesn't mean decisions are necessarily easier for you; it simply means you're naturally attuned to input that others may not notice or recognize. Still, every one of us can and will enter into discernment processes throughout our lives. Even if it doesn't come easy or naturally, we can practice being attentive by the art of reflection, through knowing and naming the reality of what is, both the discomfort and the gratitude. Over time, our ability to discern will grow, helping us to name not only the difference between lightness and darkness or goodness and corruption but also all the gradients in between. It's a way of knowing, of seeing, of moving into alignment with your truest self and your role in bringing the peace of God to the world. Binary thinking is less helpful in the process of discernment, as that implies there is always a fully right or wrong choice, direction, or decision. Instead, the process of discernment helps us to know it may be less about "right" or "wrong" and more about "near" or "far." Rather than be so concerned about a clear answer as to whether this room is the right or wrong room for me, I can ask different questions and follow the arrows where they lead.

Does staying draw me nearer to God and to people or further from God and people?

Does leaving bring me closer into alignment with my personal core values or further away?

To what degree? For how long?

What's at stake (for me and the community) if I stay?

What will I or the community lose if I leave?

With these questions in mind, I want to offer the final two movements of our PRAY acronym that will help to inform your own discernment process. We'll continue to refer to these throughout our time together.

By way of review: *P* stands for *Point and call*, the practice of naming our rooms and then asking The Ten Questions in relation to the rooms we're unsure about (see pages 31 to 35). *R* stands for *Remember your path*, recognizing that the path is behind us and our clues for moving forward can be found in personal guideposts we've already been following along the way, like our spiritual personality and personal core values (see chapter 4).

The final two movements of our PRAY discernment practice are to *Acknowledge presence* and *Yield to the arrows*.

To *acknowledge presence* is twofold. First, it's an invitation to notice and name who is with you in your particular rooms, both human and holy. As you discern your path and consider if it's time to leave a room, especially one that is dear to you, deeply rooted in you, or part of your core identity, knowing you're not alone is vital. Keep company with the Divine presence of God, the sacred presence of a spiritual companion, the love of a found community, and/or the support of family and friends. But the presence of others isn't the only one that matters. It's also equally important to acknowledge your *own* presence. This discernment process can be a lonely one, and that's true whether you're the one leaving or the one who stays. You count as company too. And it may seem counterintuitive or even strange to imagine, but you can be your own friend. In fact, you must.

In the pages that follow we'll explore four ways of acknowledging presence: reflective prayer and grounding metaphors (found later in this chapter) as well as two-word mantras and breath prayers (discussed in chapter 8). For those who just want to create a pro/con list so you can make a decision already, asking you to conjure up a grounding metaphor might feel deeply uncomfortable at best, impossibly ridiculous at worst. But discernment is a practice that involves our whole self, including our imagination. Some of my most difficult, transformative decisions have been resolved in part due to a meaningful image, picture, or metaphor that has grounded me to a deeper, sometimes invisible reality. This, too, can be a presence that comforts and sustains.

The final movement in our discernment practice is to *yield to the arrows*. When we're carrying questions about important rooms, it's easy to get lost in our heads as we try to work out what to do. That's why yielding to the arrows, rather than obsessing over answers, can be a life-giving practice in times of uncertainty. These arrows may not be obvious at first but may emerge as we engage in rhythms and rituals, both the ones in our regular life as well as the ones we create to mark endings and beginnings.

One way to stay embodied in your life as you discern your next move is to establish simple rhythms that align with your personal core values and spiritual personality. This may be as basic as taking a daily walk, keeping appointments with friends, or following a morning or evening routine. You may not know exactly what to do about a particular room quite yet, but you can follow small arrows that move you closer to your answer.

Just like rooms have scripts, so do words. And "ritual" is a word that has a lot to say. In its simplest form, ritual is another word for ceremony or an observance of something. For our purpose here, we'll use "ritual" as shorthand for marking a moment, serving as something we can either anticipate in the future or point back to in the past.

Marking the ending of things is embedded in culture. Parties, finales, weddings, birthdays, and funerals are all rituals that are also part of our regular rhythm of life. When a beginning or ending is communal, the likelihood of marking the moment increases simply because more people are involved. But just because the group marks a thing doesn't mean we own that ending for ourselves. If a beginning or ending is more personal or quiet, it might be even easier to overlook. It's important to not rush through these milestones when they come, even if the world around us doesn't recognize them. One way to do that is to find a period to end things as best we can. That's what rituals can do for us; they're a practice of marking the ending or the beginning to help us place ourselves in time, to acknowledge the gifts and burdens of the rooms we're leaving, and to honor the person we have become and are becoming.

This is important not only when we leave spaces but also when we discern it's time for us to stay. Perhaps you're questioning a particular room, you work through the four movements of PRAY, and you discern that the arrows lead you to stay. Still, something has shifted. Marking that change with a new rhythm or meaningful ritual could be an important practice for you to remain in this place where you belong for now, to do the good work required of you, and to receive renewal to carry on in what may be a less than ideal situation.

It is within the rhythms and rituals of our lives that we will find and follow the arrows of discernment. If a ritual is something we do to mark a moment, then a rhythm will be our way of life leading up to and after those moments. Our rhythm of life is an intentional way of embodying the reality of our decisions. It's a continuation on the path, a recognition that now that we've discerned our next right thing, here's how we'll live it out. While the rest of this book will bring more depth and color to these movements, what follows is one example of how acknowledging presence and yielding to arrows have accompanied me well in the midst of my own process of discernment.

While writing this book, I wrestled for months with how much to share about our exit from our church. This isn't a book about leaving church, after all, and this discernment practice isn't meant only for those looking at the rooms of faith they inhabit. The details of why and when and what happened aren't what matter here—I know this. But I also know that specificity helps when possible. And the more specific we are able to be about our own stories, the more broadly they often apply to the stories of others. It seems the opposite would be true, but nevertheless here we are. I want to share this bit because even though I know it has potential to be a distraction for some readers, for others it could be the story that saves your life. And while the details of my own story might be blurry, reality seen through a glass darkly, it's still me and I'm still living it, wanting to be as honest as I'm able while still honoring the stories that aren't fully mine to tell.

The reality of that time was this: It was June of 2020. While the world had a *shared* experience during the pandemic, we did not all have the *same* experience. Every heart knew its own pain. Like you, we had been home for three months. The kids were finishing up the end-of-the-year virtual schooling, social distancing, and seeming sadder than ever. Even though we were part of a church we loved, it was also becoming increasingly disruptive in our spirits for us to stay there. Even before the pandemic, John and I had started to wonder if our time there was nearing an end, because of both some growing theological differences as well as the anxiety that seemed to permeate the leadership and, as a result, the entire congregation. We had been paying attention to our bodies, our minds, and our hearts, each week when church was over and continued to find sadness and anger mixed together. Later I would resonate with something Beth Moore said in an interview about her exit from the Southern Baptist Convention: "It's easier to leave when you're mad than when you're sad."[3] She implied that if you wait until you're angry, you may have waited too long.

And then one day in late June, on the literal longest day of the year, I had a life-altering conversation with one of our kids. This is not my full story to tell, but what I will say is, everything you think you know about an "issue," all the theology you've been told and tried to make sense of, all the clean lines and straight edges you pointed to, none of that matters when your teenager tells you they're questioning their sexuality. What matters is the face of this beautiful soul whom you have loved into being, eyes filled with question marks, carrying the pain of anticipated rejection, wondering if they will be okay, accepted, and loved. What matters is this young life, living in secret up until now, not knowing if their very own mom would draw near or far if she knew the truth.

One thing became clear fast: our current church was not a place where our family would be able to work this out. We tried, at first. John went to lunch with the lead pastor, wanting to test the waters without revealing anything specific about our family, attempting to start a compassionate dialogue. But this pastor was either unwilling or unable to hold any nuanced space for the issue, simply restating his theological position. John wanted to build a bridge, but all this pastor could do was draw a line. This confirmed what we knew could not happen at our church even though it took some time for me to fully admit it. Still, that knowledge broke my heart.

I knew we had friends *within* the church we could talk to, and eventually we did. But the systems, structures, and leadership that made up the institution of our church at the time was simply not going to be able to hold the kind of space we were going to need, the kind that could move beyond theological arguments and doctrinal stances. We needed to receive compassion and to find hope in community. We had things to learn, stuff to process, and we needed a safe place where we could ask questions and wrestle alongside people who would handle us with care. Our kids couldn't wait for us to figure this out. We couldn't press PAUSE for two years and decide what we believed. The work that began years earlier in the parking lot that had been put aside for later was now in my living room, at my kitchen table, and deep within my heart. I know not all communities of faith will arrive at the same theological conclusions as they work to discern what God and the Bible have to say about this. I suppose the question then for you, as it was for us, becomes whether or not the rooms you're in allow for safe dialogue, wrestling, and community. Are you in a place where you feel able to disagree? Are the voices in the margins welcome at the table? Are you able to trust that God is big enough to hold it all?

For us, this felt like a life-or-death decision because it was. And while that may seem extreme, it's not an exaggeration.

According to author Bridget Eileen Rivera in her book *Heavy Burdens: Seven Ways LGBTQ Christians Experience Harm in the Church*, "religious faith reduces the risk of suicide for virtually every American demographic except one: LGBTQ people. Generations of LGBTQ people have been alienated or condemned by Christian communities."[4] I didn't know that fact at the time, but somehow I knew it in my heart. Later I got the numbers in spades.

In their 2022 National Survey on LGBTQ Youth Mental Health, the Trevor Project found that 45 percent of LGBTQ youth seriously considered attempting suicide in the last year.[5] A new CDC report released in February 2023 confirms ongoing and extreme distress among teens who identify as lesbian, gay, bisexual, or questioning (LGBQ+).[6]

We may want answers and certainty, but sometimes all we get are arrows. Arrow to the statistics that tell us who is struggling, left out, and dying. Arrow to the heartbreak of isolation and questioning. Arrow to the longing for belonging. They shout their answers and call it God, but God within me points to something different, something more vast, something that feels like mystery and sounds like love. This story is ongoing, but I'll tell you how it ends: *God is still with us.*

In the year leading up to that summer, what had started as a slow knowing came in an instant. But there was no clear path to walk when we realized it was time for us to leave our church. How does one leave a place they were once committed to cultivate and grow? Who has traveled this road that we are about to follow? Who can speak to the fear I feel, the untethering, the lack of walls? Who will normalize this free fall?

Prayer felt impossible. Everything was upside down in my inner life, like a room that was once carpeted, draped, and cozy was now mostly empty: linoleum floors, blank walls, random items left behind in a rush that are of no use to me now. The strange thing was that I was the one leaving, but the reality of my experience was I felt like the one who had been abandoned, like someone packed up all the comfortable chairs and blew out all the candles, taking with them the wax and the wicks. I wanted someone to talk to but didn't have a clue where to turn. We were leaving, but we felt left.

Of all the things we could say about 2020, one thing that was true in my experience and probably in the experience of many is that it was a year of reckoning. We all reevaluated long-held loyalties, took a deeper look at systems and structures, and learned who we can really lean on in times of difficulty.

For most all of us, many of our relied-upon tools for discernment and decision-making were altered, reduced, or completely lost to us. There was no one living to look to because we hadn't had a pandemic of this magnitude since 1920, so there was no process available. At the time, we walked forward without knowing the impact of each choice, without precedent or any assurance of a predictable result.

Our ability to be present with one another was limited or completely blocked, depriving us of the closeness we need for a sense of belonging. With the lack of shared meals or shared space, we often retreated to our homes for safety, thus cutting off communication as a result. For many, this day-to-day existence, this lack of regular routine, made it difficult to pray, if we prayed at all.

All our communal rituals were disrupted or completely eliminated that year. We were unable to mark our endings and beginnings with any degree of normalcy; births, graduations, first and last days of work, weddings, and funerals were all disrupted, altered beyond recognition, or completely canceled. Moments continued to pass without fanfare, celebration, or communal lament, endings rolling into beginnings with no one to fully bear witness to them.

The ordinary rhythms that make up our lives—commuting to work or school, seeing acquaintances in the post office or grocery store, gathering with faith communities, supper clubs, small groups, book clubs—these rhythms were halted. We couldn't plan; we couldn't forecast; we could only postpone indefinitely. We developed a habit of not counting on it and a reflex of expecting to be disappointed.

While we still walked forward in our individual lives, the lack of a global, communal path weighed heavily on us. The limited presence with people, weary and blocked imaginations, halted rituals, and unpredictable, unreliable rhythms complicated our lives in ways we couldn't articulate at the time. The types of arrows we were accustomed to looking for were lost in the fog, a spinning dial on an unfamiliar compass. Things continued to end; we continued to leave and enter various rooms of our lives without the usual points of reference. We had meetings without embodiment, experienced endings without closure, and had to practice discernment in the dark. As for John and me, it meant that our actual act of "leaving" didn't look like much. No one was attending church in person right then anyway, so it was easy to slip into the shadows, stay quiet, and disappear.

All of that was true. But as I look back at my experience of that time through the gift and practice of reflection, I now see how I made my way through the dark, how the path behind me, God's presence and the presence of others with me, and the hopeful pictures still emerged as arrows, however dim. Upon reflection, I can see how my small rituals and feeble rhythms still served as needed personal guideposts along the way.

Though I didn't know exactly what to do or how to exit, a few arrows emerged in the form of presence. One was my spiritual director. Though I'd been in the habit of seeing her monthly the eight years prior, I saw her exactly twice that year, limited because of the pandemic. But twice was not nothing, and those two visits—one via video call and the other outside on her back patio, sitting six feet apart—served as needed companionship during an upside-down time. When I felt caught up in creeds and dogma, overly focused on talking points and my own inability to put language to something I knew deep down, she reminded me: "Our vision of God can expand beyond what we've always been taught." She said, "Faith is not so much about a creedal belief but living out of the experience of who God is as revealed in the person of Jesus Christ." How could I litigate an inner knowing? How could I defend my own resolve? God's presence as experienced through the companionship of my spiritual director reminded me of love.

I had a few friends I met for walks, trading stories and sorrows of that impossible time, trying to stay socially distanced on the narrow, neighborhood trails. A couple of these friends were people who remained at the church we were in the process of leaving, and I will be forever grateful for the generous space they held for me even as they were navigating their own discernment process that led to them staying. I experienced presence in the form of my little family—three teenagers who, without the pandemical times, would have probably been gone more than they were home. The twins were old enough for their driver's licenses by now, but they had nowhere to go. In many ways, it was a dark and stressful time, filled with questions, secrets, and a slow free fall. But it was also filled with time at home, watching sitcom reruns, taking slow walks around the block, keeping our eyes on the news, and finding new ways to be together.

And then there was God, showing me a new side, an unexplored personality, a spaciousness I didn't think was possible, a host at the head of a longer table. One of the scariest parts of that summer was I didn't feel God's presence in the same way I had in the past. Being a heart-centered person who navigates the world first through feelings, then through thinking, then through action, losing that familiar sense of God was a grief I could hardly bear. But is it a real thing to say there was presence in God's absence? That the place where God was, while empty, somehow implied that God was on the move? That perhaps my theological house was being renovated, and God got up from the shelf where I had placed all things God-ish, leaving behind only an imprint surrounded by divine dust? But that dust was evidence that *God Is.* And now my work was to continue to journey and discern how God was moving now? In me, around me, still. Even now, even in the midst of my questions and uncertainty.

Something new was rising up in me, next to the fear and the doubt. It was fortitude. It was courage. It was a challenge to move forward in love even with my questions. I would not have said this then, at the time. But I can see it now, looking back, the way God moved not only through people but also through pictures informed by what I knew about the life of Jesus in the Gospel accounts. For example, rather than reading the story of Jesus feeding the five thousand and considering what this meant hermeneutically, I was more drawn to the reality that Jesus was eating with people. I was compelled by the idea of a meal with God, the wind on the hill, the sounds of the crowd, the hunger in their bellies. I was drawn to stories and imagery and started to notice how pictures would stick in my imagination more meaningfully than words in the form of what I now call "grounding metaphors." These were ideas or pictures that seemed to show up over and over in different contexts, so much so that I couldn't ignore them. I believe this was a kindness from God, a way to accompany me during a time when words were difficult, offering me a language to explore my life and questions without requiring so many words.

Here are a few of the grounding metaphors that began to emerge.

First, there was the idea of a table. N. T. Wright says this: "When Jesus wanted to explain to his followers what his death would mean, he didn't give them a theory. He gave them a meal."[7] All summer and into the fall, I couldn't shake that image of the width and length of God's table. And in my imagination, that table kept growing.

I've already shared another grounding image, one that's followed me for years: an image of fire. The fire that warms and heats, that gathers and comforts. The fire that burns at the end of a candle, marking a memory. The fire that clarifies and disrupts for the sake of something better. The fire that delights and destroys, that takes us by surprise. What kind of fire is this? That's a question I'm always asking.

Finally, one I didn't like and couldn't explain was the image of darkness—just a dark, deep unknowing. Barbara Brown Taylor's insightful book *Learning to Walk in the Dark* has been a kind companion to me along the way. "New life starts in the dark. Whether it is a seed in the ground, a baby in the womb, or Jesus in the tomb, it starts in the dark."[8]

A present absence, a table, a fire, the dark: these ordinary things of everyday life were pictures I held on to. They weren't flat, like a photograph, but images I could walk into, explore, and sit with. I paid attention when they showed up in conversation, scripture, or my own imagination. And then, late that summer, a tiny ritual emerged: I started to write haiku.

Full disclaimer: these were not in the traditional form of Japanese haiku that is meant to be a "one breath" poem connecting two seemingly unlike things together. What I did was the simplified English version, the kind we learned in middle school, with the three-line, five-seven-five syllable pattern. I broke all the haiku rules that real poets use, putting in all my filler words to hit that syllable count—not precise; still helpful. When everything stopped and all rhythms were gone, when there was no real path to follow or clear plan to depend on, when the summer blurred right into fall without a single familiar landmark, when the kids were still schooling at home with no plan to go back to a building, when my theology was turned inside out and God was silent, this tiny ritual of writing prayer-like haikus, helped.

August 14, 2020

Who are our people?
In my dark night of the soul
Fear says they'll be gone.

August 22, 2020

The Lord, my shepherd
I have everything I need.
I want to believe.

December 6, 2020

In the middle time
It's impossible to know
How things are going.

Perhaps you, too, now find yourself at a threshold wanting answers. If you're feeling stuck and aren't sure what to do next, the discernment process allows time to PRAY: *Point and call; Remember your path; Acknowledge presence; Yield to the arrows.* As you continue to look for a presence to acknowledge or an arrow to follow, one simple practice that could be a helpful rhythm to accompany you through your own questions or uncertainty is to practice praying yourself to sleep. Formally, this is most similar to the established practice of the Daily Examen, which I mentioned briefly earlier in the book. It's a form of reflective prayer for the end of the day that helps you to become aware of God's presence with you as well as to set a simple intention toward the day yet to come.

This is a practice of release, which is why I find it helpful to go through these movements in my mind once I lie down at night rather than try to write down my answers. It takes only a few minutes, and sometimes you may not even make it all the way to the end before you fall asleep. This means you've done well and the prayer is doing good work in you.

Here are five simple movements for praying yourself to sleep:

1. *Presence:* Be present in the moment, to myself and to God with me. I am here and God is here; I am now and God is now. There's nothing left to do, say, or fix today. There is only rest.

2. *Reflection:* Where did the Light of God show up in my day? As you look back over the events, conversations, movements, and moments of the day, where did you notice

the Light? Where might you have seen a glimpse of hope? A moment of gratitude? Name and notice them now.

3. *Awareness:* What feelings rise up in me now? Without judgment or agenda, simply notice how you feel as you review your day. Are you encouraged? Motivated? Exhausted? Relieved? Whatever the feeling is, notice and name it, point and call.

4. *Imagination:* Does an image or picture emerge from a particular moment of my day? Some images are just for the day; others can be carried with us for an extended period of time. In your reflection, perhaps a plant or animal you encountered today stays with you. Maybe a drawing your child brought home from school or a patch of moss you noticed on the sidewalk comes to mind. These may be pictures for the day or they could be the start of a grounding metaphor for a season. Pray from this place, asking God what you need to know.

5. *Anticipation:* Look toward tomorrow. No need to record a to-do list or an agenda. Simply settle in where you are, offer a simple gratitude for it, and look ahead into tomorrow, trusting that whatever has emerged that you need will remain with you and whatever emerged that you don't need will fall away into God's care.

This simple five-movement prayer can be a tiny ritual all by itself, helping to loosen your grip on what shred of control you may think you have and allow the moments of difficulty, embarrass-ment, uncertainty, or confusion to sit tight in the lap of God while you sleep. It may also serve as a way to access a grounding metaphor for this particular season of change, one that is rooted not in the life you thought should be but in the life you are actually living.

Peace or Avoidance

Listen, are you breathing just a little, and calling it a life?

—MARY OLIVER, "HAVE YOU EVER TRIED TO
ENTER THE LONG BLACK BRANCHES?"

The beginning of 2021 felt like one giant hallway. John and I were several months into the realization that it was time for us to leave our church, and I was at peace about that decision in my mind, but we hadn't made anything official. As we rang in the new year and I reflected on the twelve preceding months, I realized that the last time we had attended church before everything shut down was in early March 2020. But we didn't know the last time was the last time.

So many of us have had lasts we didn't know were lasts, either because of those pandemic years or because of other unexpected circumstances outside of our control. This can be one reason it's difficult to move on. There was no marking a final moment, no acknowledgment of the end. There was no deep breath before the last gathering, no meaningful journal entry afterward, no slide-show look-back, no tearful conversations or well-wishing hugs. For us in the early spring of 2020, there was just a regular Sunday where we ate donut holes before finding our seats on the left-hand side toward the back like always. It was my turn to read scripture that week, so I did so from the pulpit before the sermon. We sang along with piano and guitar to familiar, comforting songs. I'm sure I saw friends from a distance and didn't make an effort to walk over to say hello, thinking I would just catch them next week. And then next week turned into never.

That is sometimes the reality of our endings, and certainly happened for a lot of us during 2020. No foreshadowing, no runway, no warning. Just regular life straight into an abrupt ending. For anyone who left or was left that year, for anyone who lost someone they loved that year, for anyone who was let go from a job or lost their home or moved away, the unformed endings just faded into our lives, without boundaries or markings. The endings we got were nothing like the endings we always imagined would be (if we imagined the endings at all).

John and I had countless conversations at our kitchen table, on the sofa in the evening, on hundreds of walks around the block. We processed and overprocessed the whole thing. We confided in a few dear friends who were still at the church, and they knew why we could no longer stay. We also processed with friends who had discerned it was time for them to leave as well, like my friend Anna. (As it turns out, it's unlikely that either of our kids will be married in that beautiful sanctuary after all.) But when it came to actually walking away, I thought we could just quietly disappear, thought we would avoid being seen as people who cause trouble, who leave angry, who raise hell on the way out. *We'll just stay quiet and leave in peace. We won't make anyone feel uncomfortable.* Plus, we were still working to hold our child's story with care, not wanting to share things that simply weren't ours to share. Sometimes a quiet leaving is appropriate, necessary even. But for me, it was only after some time, several weeks into the new year, that I began to realize the toll this non-ending was having on my body and the shallow definition of peace I was holding on to.

On the day of the presidential inauguration in January 2021, we turned on the live coverage to witness history and the peaceful transfer of power. The kids were all home doing virtual school, so their schedule was flexible. We watched the whole ceremony, from the Invocation to Lady Gaga singing the national anthem to the swearing in of the vice president and the president. I had my laptop open to the presidential website to make note of the exact moment when it would reflect a new administration. I'm fascinated by these reverential ceremonies and all the planning and organizing that go into them, all the people behind the scenes required to pull off an event like this. It's remarkable to imagine everything that happens in the five-hour window the staff has to move one presidential family out of the White House and the new one in. I read that because of security reasons, they can't hire outside movers to do the job, so everyone from the staff florist to the White House chef is involved in the flip, making it so one First Family wakes up in the White House in the morning, and by the evening the new one is settled in, down to their favorite brand of shampoo placed in the shower. If they would let us watch that transition in real time, it would be must-see TV for me. But that day, I settled for marking the moment the website flips, so I sat there with my laptop, continuously refreshing the page. At 11:59 a.m. Eastern Standard Time, just after his swearing in, the website switched from the office of the former president to the office of the newly inaugurated president.

"There it is!" John said it with a smile, briefly interested because he knew I was, casually watching over my shoulder. The new president delivered his inaugural address and then, shortly after that, a young woman in a bright yellow coat and a red headband took the stage. The chyron said her name was Amanda Gorman, age twenty-two, the youngest poet laureate in inaugural history. She wrote a poem specifically for the inauguration called "The Hill We Climb." And in the midst of multitasking on my computer, with the kids eating lunch and John disciplining the dog in the background, as soon as she began to speak, I was riveted to my TV screen. Her words were clear, her small hands delicate and dancing as she recited them.

I grabbed on to one of the lines of her poem immediately and shared it on Instagram within five minutes of her leaving the stage. I could tell it was resonating, and of course I wasn't the only one sharing her words. Then I found myself refreshing another page, this time her Instagram account. I watched as Gorman's follower count rose by ten thousand every minute, people doing what I was doing, listening to her in real time, then finding her on Instagram to learn who she was. By the end of the day, she had over one million followers. Clearly her words resonated with a lot of people. But there was one line she said, tucked in near the beginning, and this one I wasn't as quick to re-share or highlight. This one was for me to carry, to handle, to turn over and over in my hands and heart.

> *We've learned that quiet isn't always peace,*
> *And the norms and notions of what "just is"*
> *Isn't always justice.*[1]

Gorman's poem had a particular point of view and was written for a particular moment in time and I want to honor that for what it is, for what it represents and what she was calling out. That is true, and also, in her specificity, we can all relate to the universal truth she articulated. *Quiet isn't always peace*. And there it was. She named something I needed to hear, put words to her own experience, and the experience of history, and named something for my current experience too. As I sat there on my sofa, listening to this young woman recite her own crafted words, the smallest path opened up for me, the tiniest arrow pointing to what to do next. In this decision to leave our church, we were remaining mostly quiet. But in our silence, I realized we were communicating that there was peace, when in reality, there was none. If there was a third way, one that didn't require either raising hell or staying quiet, I wanted to find it.

There is a difference between the peace that comes from doing the deeply right thing and the relief that comes from avoiding discomfort. Looking back, I can now name that I was conflating the peace

I felt about making the decision to leave (a true peace) with the method in which we were choosing to do it (avoiding discomfort). Translation: my plan was to just sort of disappear. I thought we could experience the benefit and relief of leaving without having to face the pain of actually, well, *leaving*.

While the decision itself might be the exact right thing for you, the method matters. In fact, sometimes the method is the thing that causes the most confusion, heartbreak, and pain, even more than the leaving itself. Breaking up by text, ghosting a friend without explanation, quitting a job without notice—these are all circumstances where the decision to exit the room may be well-founded but the method by which you choose to exit could cause more harm than the leaving itself. There is no way to speak to every nuanced situation in a medium like this, and so it bears saying and repeating: sometimes the only way to leave is to disappear, to walk away without explanation or conversation. It's not always possible to leave well, however you interpret that term. Like Gorman says, *quiet isn't always peace*, but sometimes quiet *is* peace. We all have to discern for ourselves when the simplest goodbye is needed, when we need to hold onto our peace by remaining silent, or when we need to speak all the way out. That's why it's worth exploring what leaving well looks like *for you*. We want to give ourselves our best chance at closure, at healing, and at eliminating the things that are within our sphere of control that could cause more harm than is necessary.

This faux peace can show up in other ways during the discernment process. If you consider the rooms you're in and you imagine a confrontation that might come as a result of your decision or the resistance you'll likely get if they know you've changed your mind, it's natural that you would begin to have a sense of fear and discomfort. But that fear and discomfort are often interpreted as a closed door or even a wall. They could be that, but they're not necessarily that. Fear and discomfort aren't usually answers by themselves but are often arrows: important to pay attention to, but it's also best to ask yourself what they're pointing to. At first, it helps to consider them as yellow flags meant to slow you down rather than assume they are red flags every time. The question to discern is if the fear and discomfort are pointing to a wall (*Don't go this way*), a window (*Here's something that's possible*), a mirror (*This is a time for self-reflection*), or a door (*Yeah, it's time to go*).

We may tend to assume that fear is a sign that we're moving in the wrong direction. *I don't feel peace about it. Abort mission! I'm staying put!* It's possible to stay in a room too long or to rush out too fast because we're paying attention to a narrow set of cues. Our definition of peace, in this case, means the absence of fear or anxiety.

True peace is not the absence of discomfort or conflict.

True peace is an inner okay-ness and wholeness.

True peace is an alignment with what we know and what we do, living in congruence with our personal core values, our true identity, the common good, and our life with God. But any kid who has ever had braces knows that getting things into alignment almost always includes discomfort.

So how can we even begin to discern the difference between true peace and discomfort avoidance? I asked Dr. Hillary L. McBride this question on *The Next Right Thing* podcast. She is a therapist and researcher who specializes in embodiment and is also the author of the book *The Wisdom of Your Body*. She pointed out the importance of that question. "What is a peace about something and what is us trying to get away from something that's hard? We feel relief because we're avoidant. [That is] actually how the anxiety cycle works for most people in our colloquial understanding . . . but this anxiety responsive activation is fueled by us leaving or withdrawing or avoiding things that are scary for us, which serves to only increase our anxiety around it when we approach that thing again. We confuse the relief of leaving with the right thing to do, and we don't realize that it's actually our body getting a break from the anxiety of facing the thing that we learned was scary, but isn't scary."

She then went on to use an example of the social anxiety some of us feel going to a party. It feels scary, so we leave. And when we leave, we feel better. This seems to prove to our nervous system that we can't handle the party. If we go to another party, it may feel even scarier, which means our reward for leaving is even greater. This could be an example of experiencing faux peace. It doesn't mean leaving was the right thing to do or that we were actually in any danger. It just means our nervous system felt relieved when we left.

She then issued an invitation to pay attention to our bodies. "Being able to tell the difference between what is the relief that comes from my avoidance and what is actually peace is a whole life's work. . . . They will show up differently if you hold them side by side. If you know those sensations enough and you're familiar with them enough, you will be able to tell the difference. But for most of us, we don't have a fine-tooth comb that we can move through those different sensations to be able to tell. It's very easy to confuse them."[2] We won't be able to complete that work in one chapter, but we can explore what it means to begin that work now.

First, it's good to remember what we mean by "peace," and what it means to be well. "To be 'well,'" according to authors Emily Nagoski and Amelia Nagoski in their book *Burnout: The Secret to Unlocking the Stress Cycle*, "is not to live in a state of perpetual safety and calm, but to move fluidly from a state of adversity, risk, adventure, or excitement, back to safety and calm, and out again. Stress is not bad for you; *being stuck* is bad for you."[3] We're meant to move in and out of stress, not to stay stuck in a room of perceived safety. We're meant to move to the healthy, human rhythm of leaving rooms and finding new ones. This can cause stress, to be sure. But stress doesn't automatically mean we're not well.

In Hebrew scripture, the word translated into English as peace is "shalom." It means to make restitution and to restore. It also implies an overall sense of wholeness or completeness, *to be full of well-being*. This is the kind of peace we long for, the kind that is an outcome of being deeply okay, not necessarily because all is well without but because all is well within. This is an inner kind of peace, an inner knowing and receiving peace with God and a desire to impart peace in the world.

If you notice anxiety coming at you as you hold the question of whether or not it's good for you to stay in a room or if it's time to leave, rather than interpreting the anxiety as a red flag, warning you to turn around in order to avoid the fear and discomfort, are you willing to hold the tension just a little bit longer? Let's begin to apply the movements we've learned so far, starting with a point-and-call practice. I'll narrate a possible dialogue happening in your mind:

When I consider either staying here longer or leaving this room, I experience discomfort, fear, anxiety, dread, and a desire to escape this decision. In the past I may have interpreted this as a sign that I was moving in the wrong direction and would seek out feelings of peace and safety as a result. But now I want to discern the difference between true peace and discomfort avoidance.

A similar dialogue was running through my mind when I imagined having to articulate our reasons for leaving or to have a conversation with the leaders of our church. When we first got married, John was on staff at another church for twelve years. We know how easy it is for people to be critical and how difficult (and even rare) it is to stick around to effect change. During those years, we understood the discouragement and frustration that comes from being on the receiving end of complaints, unfair assumptions, and anonymous letters. So imagining the work of articulating our reasons for leaving felt uncomfortable for many reasons, but one of them was we respect the role of pastor and we knew our reasons had less to do with one person or group of people and more to do with a whole system. This was harder to confront or articulate, which made it more compelling to avoid.

Back to our practice.

As we pause to name what's happening within and around us, rather than assume our uncomfortable physical and emotional response is an automatic red flag, let's consider it to be a yellow flag for now, meant to slow us down, to invite attention, and to tend to our posture as we make our decision.

Here is where Ignatian spirituality provides us with helpful language in naming our posture, or the direction we're facing as we make decisions, with the concepts of *consolation* and *desolation*.

"Consolation" is a word that describes our spiritual state, including a feeling that draws us toward God and others. It's when we feel an increase in faith, hope, or love that leads us to peace. An experience of consolation may also include sadness or grief over a circumstance, but it's the kind of sadness and grief that draws us near to God.

Desolation is another category of feeling, in which our focus is turned in on ourselves, drawing us away from the love of God or of others. Some may describe this as a spiritual dryness or lethargy, a lack of motivation toward goodness, and an absence of the felt presence of God. When we're in a state of desolation, we may feel pulled down into a spiral of negative feelings and want to give up on things that were once important to us.

Note that these are not static states of elation and despair, and they aren't in any way diagnostic or psychological terms. These are simply ways to describe and talk about an inner state of being that we may move in and out of all the time in daily life. No need to place morality labels on them, as consolation and desolation are part of the human experience. But the work of naming them can serve as informative arrows for us as we consider the state of our inner life when we're working to discern if it's time to leave a room or enter a new one. What's happening beneath the surface of our life as we consider a particular decision to stay or to go has an impact on our ability to make a move from the deepest part of who we are.

Being able to name our inner experience of consolation or desolation can be one useful way to put language to our current posture.

Back to our established PRAY-er practice of pointing and calling, remembering our path, acknowledging presence, and yielding to arrows.

As you engage with God from your own spiritual personality, what do you notice? Does this action (or non-action) align with your personal core values? Is someone present who you can turn to, seek counsel from, or sit with in prayer and listening? Is there an image that you've been carrying that informs your next move? Is there a next step you can take that aligns with what you value most?

Hold your answers to these questions before you. If you sense discomfort, is your aversion to that action a result of setting a healthy boundary or avoiding an uncomfortable confrontation? Is your fear coming from a solid place of wisdom, because to take this action would actually threaten your safety? Or is the fear coming from a more tender place, one that desperately wants to avoid disruption?

Here's the thing. When I get quiet and honest with myself, I know the difference. Beneath all my explanations, excuses, and defenses, at the core of who I am, from the same place where I heard my friend Jesus say to me, *When they walk out, you follow them*, I can hear other things too. Not audibly, and sometimes not as clearly. But there is an inner knowing that the wind cannot touch, the fire cannot burn, the waters cannot overcome. There is a solid, still place deep within us where we dwell as whole. And from that place we can discern if our fear is a healthy fear, a result of wisdom. Or if our fear is a dysfunctional fear, a result of avoidance.

When John and I sat with the reality of having left our church but not really telling anyone, when I held that out before me and considered what it meant to walk into the hallway, I just knew I couldn't leave and move on to something new in freedom until we at least tried to articulate why we were leaving. And so we decided to write a letter.

There's a long history of people remaining silent in the name of "peace" and subsequently perpetuating harm. In the scope of life, our decision to write a letter was the smallest thing, the tiniest declaration. But our quiet wasn't peace. Saying something imperfectly, we decided, would be better than nothing at all.

We wrote a few drafts, but nothing felt quite right. We were still getting used to our own voice in this. How do you tell the truth without blaming or sounding petty or being overly defensive or overly offensive or, or, or? So the first draft didn't lie, but it also didn't tell the truth. We wrote a second and a third.

We did our best. We were going through the biggest shift of faith in our lives, asking questions we hadn't been brave enough to ask before, wanting to be wise, thoughtful, and faithful people. We desperately wanted to communicate that we hadn't lost our minds, that we were desperate for God. Most of all, our concern was for our kids. And we felt utterly alone. I wanted more than anything to be able to run into the arms of the leadership and community at our church and say, "Hey, guys, we're navigating something new with our kiddo that we didn't know before, something nuanced but also confusing. It might be beautiful. We hope it's beautiful. Can we trust you to walk with us through it? To love and accept them no matter what? To demonstrate the love of God to our family? Will you hold us in our grief? In our confession? Will you make space for us, confess alongside us? Would you be willing to hear us out, to hold questions without answers? Would you be willing to take a second look? Would you be with us? Would you stay with us?"

But we didn't say any of that. We had enough evidence to know that this was not a place that would be able to do that for us, at least not in our experience. We told the truth, but not the whole truth. We extended gratitude and said some of what we felt. If I had it to do over again, I would have said things differently, done things differently. But we don't get to do endings over again. We do our best, we fight for the closure we need at the time and trust it's enough for now.

After they received our letter, one of the leaders in the church reached out and requested a meeting, to hear us out and listen if we wanted to say more. We said yes and ended up meeting with two kindhearted elders who listened to our swan song on a cold March night. We were honest, sometimes brutally so. We shared a lot, but not everything.

Even without all the details, to their great credit, they listened without defensiveness. They were patient and bighearted, took notes and asked questions. Toward the end of our time, when they asked us where we'd decided to attend church, we shocked both them and ourselves by bursting into tears, which for me isn't really rare, but coming from John, this was a complete surprise. Because we didn't know. And now that we had officially left our church, we had to face the reality of this painful unknowing. Who would receive us? Where could we go? Was there any place to belong? We felt so desperately alone.

I wish we'd said more—not necessarily just at the end but along the way. I own that and have made peace with my silence. Not only in this situation but also when I reflect on my whole life, there are times I wish I had said more, done more. I wish I had spoken up more often for those in the margins. I wish I had known sooner the pain and rejection so many people feel inside the walls of the church. I wish I had confronted my own silence in so many areas of life sooner. And I wish I had admitted what I knew deep down: that quiet isn't always peace.

But I'm learning now. I've grown in my understanding of myself as a leader. I've pointed at and called to my gift of discernment. There's a knowing that runs like a rushing current within, the place where your spirit and God's meet in union. From here, I'm learning to live and move and have my being. But I haven't arrived, and that's okay.

If you get it wrong, it's okay too. You haven't wrecked it up. I firmly believe that beginning a practice of paying attention to this nuance is worth the work, even if it means we stay too long or leave too soon. I believe when we are willing to say "Is this true peace or is it the relief that comes from avoidance?" that just asking the question is good work and sets us on a path toward goodness and healing. Even when fear holds us back, God holds us up, stands by us and with us. And the truth is, we're still gonna be okay.

If you travel to Israel today, you may hear "shalom" as both a word of greeting when you enter and as a blessing when you leave. "Shalom," holding both blessing and benediction, a word to meet us as we cross over thresholds; peace as we enter in and as we walk out, a greeting and a farewell. May it be so, within us, around us, and among us.

8

Readiness or Timeliness

*There are some people who leave early, and others
who have a tendency to overstay, and I am an
overstayer of the most extreme kind and have lived
that way for most of my life. One of the most central
learnings of midlife is learning how to let go.*

—SHAUNA NIEQUIST, *I GUESS
I HAVEN'T LEARNED THAT YET*

Since 1975, NBC has aired the same show on the same day at
the same time—*Saturday Night Live*—making it one of the
longest running programs in television history. For nearly
fifty years, this show has been a consistent fixture, a landmark of
NBC programming. The sheer volume of activity, planning, and
personnel it takes to pull off this show every week for this long is
remarkable. Consider just the portion of the show that includes pre-
recorded pieces. Tuesday through Saturday, the production sched-
ule is a mix of organized chaos. That's when they record those

segments that will run during the live show, allowing them to include more ambience and special effects that wouldn't work as well live. This began with commercial parodies and then expanded to include the production of elaborate short films. In those early days they would do just ten shorts a year, but in recent years they have up to three units working on short films every single week, full-scale.

On Mondays, they figure out the promo they will film on the following day with the host (an actor, comedian, or musician, different every week). They shoot the promo on Tuesdays and then hustle to edit and mix so it can air on TV that night to tease Saturday's show. On Wednesdays they read through ten or twelve scripts and choose two or three to actually film. Immediately, they have to make costume, set, and design decisions for each script. Once decisions are made, sets are built and locations are scouted. Next are rewrites, new jokes pitched, edits made by the writers. (It's still Wednesday.) Bear in mind, one changed line of dialogue could require a new prop at least, or even an entire set change. Thursdays they work out the schedule, budget, and logistics. On Fridays, hundreds of people work overnight to build sets in preparation for filming in three different locations across the city. As soon as the shoots wrap, post-production takes over and the show editors work with the producers to ensure they're focusing on the right things. And then on Saturday, no matter what, something has to air. The editors and producers work all day alongside the people doing visual effects. And then they have the dress rehearsal where they show the clips to a live audience. Based on their reactions as well as the reactions of the show's creators, they may still have things to change, effects to add, or scenes to cut. By now it's 10 p.m. on Saturday night. Sometimes scenes make it to air with missing special effects, accidental green screens, or random cuts in wrong places.[1] They do incredible work, but in a war between timing and readiness, timing will always win. In her book *Bossypants*, Tina Fey repeated what show creator Lorne Michaels often said: "The show doesn't go on because it's ready; it goes on because it's 11:30."[2] Anyone who has ever had to hit a deadline knows this reality. Unlike math, when it's clear that the work is either done or not done, creative work is never really finished. It's simply *due*. It's not about readiness; it's about timeliness.

Whether we're facing an ending because of an anticipated, forced, or chosen goodbye, this tension between readiness and timeliness is an important one to point to, call out, and name. Knowing the difference and how these two concepts play, influence, and interact with each other could be helpful in our continued practice of discernment.

If you've ever expected a baby, you know the panic of *It's time, but I'm not ready*, like I felt when the twins came seven weeks early. And if you've ever experienced that acute, piercing pain for a child but biology or circumstance prevented it from happening, you know the heartbreak of being fully ready but it never being time. In both examples, though, the timing is mostly out of our hands. But in our decision-making lives, we have to make a choice and discern for ourselves, with God, and with our people, whether or not the time has come and whether or not we're ready.

There isn't just one way to measure readiness, but when you're ready, your whole body knows it and sometimes shows it. Readiness might look like leaning forward, bags packed, foot tapping, hands fidgety. Readiness is on your mark, get set, and ready to go. Sometimes readiness shows up calm and steady, a deep down knowing, a solid center. You might experience a freedom or release you haven't experienced before, bringing a dawn of unfolding awareness that you are, in fact, ready to make a move, a decision, or a change. Readiness may also show up like a bone-deep tiredness, an exhaustion you can't put word language to, a fed-up-ness that has no capacity to hold another drop of hardship. You are ready. But is it time?

The readiness and timeliness that is easiest to discern is the kind that comes with anticipated endings, when you've had a date marked on the calendar for years, circled in red and starred in gold. No discernment is needed to mark it because the time is a date and everyone knows it: time to graduate, deploy, retire, get married. This is when you're mostly ready (because are we ever fully, 100 percent ready?), and also, it's time.

Sometimes you get told it's time and it takes you by surprise. You didn't have time to plan or prepare for this and you certainly are not ready. But it's still time. Time may arrive obviously with a stroke of the clock or the day of the deadline. But our bodies know about timeliness too.

From our earliest days, we learn the impact of "Ready or not, here I come," with the childhood game of hide-and-seek, when you second-guess your choice of hiding place, when you grab that throw blanket off the sofa and cover yourself last-minute, hoping it's enough to conceal your small frame at least long enough for the seeker to find someone else first. In our young bodies, we experienced a simple and embodied timeliness, trying not to wet our pants, stifling a laugh, peeking around the corner to see what might be coming next. Maybe we didn't find the best place to hide, but time was up, ready or not. Timeliness is sending kids to school for the first time in kindergarten or dropping them off at college. Timeliness was me in Grandma Morland's cluttered, windowless bathroom, one last visit before climbing into the moving truck packed to the brim on our way to our new home in Iowa. Timeliness was writing a letter to the leaders of our church, not because we knew exactly what to say or even because we felt ready to write it but just because we had waited long enough and knew we couldn't move fully forward without this one last word, however small and imperfect it was. Timeliness is eleven thirty on a Saturday night.

What we mostly hope is for readiness and timeliness to align. Like a grand retirement party after forty years of faithful service, we're often looking for this kind of poetic permission to leave one room and enter a new one. You're ready and it's time. Thanks be to God, no discernment required. Of course you might have to navigate feelings of sadness or questions about what's next, but you're not confused about whether or not you're meant to leave this room. Some endings happen this way, and when they do, I hope you wrap your beautiful arms around those meaningful moments and breathe in every last celebratory part of them. Take photos, give toasts, cry big sappy tears for the gratitude of it all.

For most of us, most of the time, we get one without the other. And when we do, the gap between readiness and timeliness shows up as nerves, anticipation, sometimes excitement and joy, other times fear and grief. We may confuse our lack of feeling ready with the reality of it being time. Or we think it must not be time simply because we don't feel ready. Sometimes this is what keeps us in rooms. We feel tension when we're ready to go but it isn't yet time. And we often experience fear when it's time to go but we don't feel ready.

As we yield to the arrows of discernment, some tiny rituals that could help along the way are simple breath prayers and two-word mantras.

I'm ready but it isn't time. *How can I know if it's time?* The short answer is, you might not know *for sure*. But you can know *for now*. This is my most loved and used two-word mantra. I use "mantra" quite loosely in this context, simply as a statement repeated frequently. When I'm fully ready but it isn't quite time, I repeat this phrase as a reminder, an arrow, and a prayer. *For now* reminds me that it won't always be this way, that I can endure because this has an end date. I may not know exactly when the time will be right, but when I look at the path behind me, I can point out and call to moments when I was ready but it wasn't time. Until eventually, it was. *For now* is an arrow, pointing at the place where I now stand, keeping me in this present moment. They are two words that, when added to what feels like an impossible sentence, can take away the implied assumption of *forever* and can shift my focus ever so slightly to this right-now moment, which is the only one I have.

My kids are struggling *for now*.

I'm working overtime *for now*.

I'm missing an outlet for creativity *for now*.

We don't have a faith community *for now*.

I don't know what I'm doing *for now*.

I feel like I don't belong *for now*.

Finally, *for now* can be a prayer, an acceptance of what is and a trust that we are not alone in it. Bringing all our for-nows to God can serve as both a confession and a relief: *I don't have any answers; I can't control outcomes; I need a source outside of myself to accompany me in this interim space.* I've even used these two words as a foundation for a simple breath prayer, which is an ancient form of contemplative prayer that coincides with your inhale and exhale. Also called "prayers of the heart," breath prayers are not fancy or fussy but are a way to remember God is with us wherever we go, as close as the air around us and within us. You can choose a lyric, a line of scripture, a poem, a phrase, a word, or a mantra.

If you're feeling ready but it isn't yet time, here are some breath prayers you can borrow, for along the way:

(Inhale) For now
(Exhale) I will wait.

(Inhale) For now
(Exhale) I'm held in love.

(Inhale) For now I fear not
(Exhale) for you are with me.

It's time, but I'm not ready. What if the opposite is true? *I know it's time, but I'm nowhere near ready.* Rather than a practice of patience, we're invited into a practice of courage. During that summer of 2020, I was 0 percent ready to answer the kinds of questions our kids were asking about God, about themselves, about church, and about the world. I wasn't ready to face the reality of systemic racism in our country and how it had infiltrated systems I was part of, but it was past time to do it. I wasn't ready to consider the ways the church (*my church*) had contributed to harming those in the LGBTQ+ community but it was time to do it. I wasn't ready to leave behind a church I still loved. But my readiness didn't matter. It was time. And so I learned to move forward even though I wasn't ready, even though I wished I had more time, even though I didn't feel equipped or prepared.

The same tiny rituals helped here as well: breath prayers and two-word mantras. In the same way that *for now* helped me make a small bit of peace with it not being time, *let go* helps me make peace with not feeling ready. It bears noting that *let go* may encompass the best and the worst of us. At our worst, I fear we've spiritually bypassed our way to a sneaky accusation and an impossible goal. *Just let go and let God. Trust and release!* Yeah? Well, exactly how am I supposed to do that? It may be an easy thing to say but takes a lifetime of work to learn to do. Let's stop shaming ourselves for holding on when we know we "should" be letting go.

Let go of my insistence that I'm supposed to know everything.

Let go of the idea of what entering this room is supposed to look like.

Let go of the image of what a smarter, more equipped parent should say or be.

Let go of the expectation that I should feel better, worse, more peace, more anger in any certain situation.

Let go of my idea of what I think readiness should look like.

Let go is an invitation to *let be what is*, and to release my hold on the outcome. *Let go* is not a rule or a scolding but is a fluid invitation. If it feels impossible to let go for any extended period of time, it can even be combined with another now-familiar two-word mantra: *let go for now*, for this minute in time, where I am right now.

When you're ready but it isn't time, add *for now*.

When it's time but you're not ready, add *let go*.

Here is where a breath prayer can save the day, and the following are a few breath prayers you can borrow if you don't feel ready but the time has come.

> (Inhale) Let in what is.
> (Exhale) Let go what isn't.
>
> (Inhale) I receive you.
> (Exhale) I believe you.
>
> (Inhale) Let go
> (Exhale) for now.

You might find different two-word mantras to be helpful depending on your situation:

> *Not yet.*
> *Wait well.*
> *Stay here.*
> *Be brave.*

I'm good.

Me too.

Lean in.

Rest well.

Keep going.

For me.

Look again.

Grow slow.

There's no wrong mantra. From here, you can write your own breath prayers using these two-word mantras or ones you choose yourself.

I'm not ready and it's not time. A few final words for those rooms where all is well, where you mostly fit and it mostly fits and no discernment is needed to stay or go because you know you're right where you need to be—that's when there's no need to be ready because it's not time. You are where you are and you're good to be there. Or at least you're content to be there for now.

Same goes for **I'm ready and it's time,** like for those anticipated endings, those moments of clarity, those deep down knowings that the time is right to make a change, a move, or a decision to leave. A generative two-word mantra for when readiness and timeliness align is simple: *Thank you.*

It's 2013, and I sit in the back seat of an airport shuttle on my way to speak at a conference in Austin, Texas. In the shuttle with me is my friend Melissa, who is traveling with me, and a well-known author and pastor who is speaking at the same conference. This is the first time I've met him in person, though I've read at least one of his books. We are essentially strangers, but we fall into easy conversation around common ground, namely writing and ministry. As we ride from the airport to the hotel, he asks a few questions and I end up sharing with him about our stage of life. I tell him about John leaving youth ministry just a few months earlier after twelve years of service. I tell him about how John has chosen a stay-at-home life, the changing-sheets and doing-laundry and planning-meals kind of life, and how he's good for now, but he's open and listening for what kind of work might be next. I tell him about how I love writing books but I'm not sure what that means five or ten years from now. And really, I could do that kind of work from anywhere. So what does that mean about where we call home? I have a million questions I'm not asking out loud. He seems to know this. He seems to sense the questions beneath, and he smiles before he says this line that I will never forget: "You're in the ellipsis."

Immediately two things happen. One, I know he's right. And two, I don't want to be here, in the ellipsis. I'm ready to be in the middle of the paragraph, in the middle of the book where I know the title and the subtitle and the back cover copy. In that moment I realize how desperately I want my life to be written in ink, filled out, formed, and finished. *What in the world is next?*

I listen as he begins to tell his own story and says how he's been at the same church for seventeen years and he hopes to stay there until he retires. This is a foreign language to me. Up to this point, John and I have never felt this way about a church, a home, or a job.

Here in the seat of an airport shuttle next to Melissa and our new friend, I realize maybe for the first time that I want to feel about our life and our work and our home the way he feels about his. I want to be so committed to a local church and a job and a home that I would say with confidence, "I could stay here forever." I was ready for a sure thing. But it was not time.

That ride from the airport to the hotel was ten years ago now. I've still never experienced that "I could stay here forever" feeling I was hoping for at that time in my life. Now, instead of trying to find a place to call home forever, or a job or a church or a particular creative expression, I'm learning that even though the places and spaces that surround our lives may change over time, one place I want to be content to stay forever is with myself.

Here are a few things I know for sure:

I know that being confident about what you want to do or where you want to be does not guarantee you'll get it any more than being unsure guarantees you won't.

I know that it's possible to be rooted, even if you're in motion, just as it's possible to be scattered, even if you're staying in one place.

I know that having doubts and questions about what you want to do or where you want to live or who you hope to become does not mean you don't have a home.

I know that finding where you belong is not a onetime decision, and uncovering your belonging is slow, important work.

In her book *Placemaker*, Christie Purifoy writes: "Home is never simply a threshold you cross. It's a place you make and a place that might make—or unmake—you."[3] I'm paying attention to my everyday spaces, like the place where I type on my computer at my house.

For years our back bedroom has been a guest room, and half of that time it's doubled as my office. But guests don't stay with us very often. And I realized I was squeezing into the corner of the room with a too-small desk that I used every single day in order to make space for a guest room bed that was used twice a year. So we took out that bed and we made a place for my work in that guest room. I turned it into an office because I decided to take a second look and be honest about what was really going on here and what was the place I really needed to make. It's in the same place it was before, but now it has more of a purpose. It's not fancy and it's certainly not expensive, but making that space felt like a declaration: "This work is important. You're in this for the long haul." That's not to say we'll be here forever. It's to say we're here *for now*, so let's make a place for the work we feel compelled to do.

As I reflect on these small movements, the gift of place-making rises up to meet me, because long ago in the back seat of an Austin airport shuttle, I longed for the rootedness I heard in that pastor's voice, the surety, the face set like a flint in the direction of home, of a people and of a place. Now I see how the answer to that longing is all around me. It didn't come swiftly, it didn't come all at once, and there are still some things I'm ready for even though it's not yet time. Still, it's important to notice and to name what's here, what has gone before, and what I hope for later.

What I longed for in that airport shuttle is what I've longed for often since then, and I'm sure you can relate: surety, rootedness, and a promise that I had found my place once and for all. What I've discovered and am still discovering in the ten years since is that even though it goes against everything we've learned about plants, roots are something we can take with us wherever we go. Home isn't something we have to wait for. Home is a place we can make—even as we carry questions, even when we don't feel ready, even as we leave beloved rooms, even while we stand in various hallways. When I'm feeling small, scattered, unsure, or disconnected, I've found place-making to be a grounding practice. Breath prayers and two-word mantras are a practical way to do that right where we are.

Sometimes you're ready, but it's not time. Other times it's time, but you don't feel ready. And so when it's time and I'm ready, I'm learning to be grateful for alignment, and to pay attention to the gifts the moment offers.

If you're in the ellipsis in your own life right now, it's true: you might have more questions than you have answers. You might have more furrowed brows than nodding heads. But there are some things you can still choose, like making a place where your roots are lacking, like believing for sure that God is with you, like doing your next right thing in love. So you continue to point and call, to move forward in recollection along the path you've followed to get where you are now, and continue to move into the hallway.

Here's to knowing you're not the only one even if the people around you seem to have all found their place already.

Here's to being honest about what is true today.

Here's to not looking too far into the future or living too far in the past.

Here's to grieving and celebrating and grieving again.

Here's to experiencing the life of Christ in new and unexpected ways.

Here's to a longer table, even if, for now, it's only in your heart.

Endings and Closure

I pray that your body gets all that it needs
and if you don't want healing, I just pray for peace.

—SPENCER LaJOYE, "PLOWSHARE PRAYER"

A common question is: "What would you grab in a fire?" It used to be the family photo albums, but that's no longer as necessary as it once was, with all our photos floating around in the cloud. We still have things we think we'd grab if the house was burning down, but in the urgency of the moment, probably we'd end up with something random, something near the door on the way out, or nothing at all. When we're leaving rooms or entering new ones, some things we can bring with us and other things we will need to leave behind. Before we can even name what those things are, we have to acknowledge that something has ended, either because we're the one who left or we're the one who stayed behind.

Maybe it ended abruptly and there was no time to recognize it, much less grieve or celebrate it. Perhaps it ended badly and it was too painful to look at, so you don't. Or maybe life just got busy. Yes, you met the goal, reached the finish line, left the room, or were left behind, but there was dinner to make and errands to run and you never had a chance to mark the moment. You've been unwilling, unable, or maybe simply unaware that you needed to put a period on an ending. Maybe it's even been years. You just kept on going without acknowledging the room, what happened there, what's happening in you, both the gifts and the burdens. Whether it's an anticipated goodbye or an honest admission that things just aren't working out with a job, a person, a role, or a project; whether this new parting is something you chose or something placed upon you by circumstance, it might be tempting to either rush past this ending to the next thing or to wallow in shame, discouragement, or heartbreak over how it ended. Rather than indulging the extremes of either ignoring it or perseverating over what happened, here's a third way: take back the narrative. The ending does not define the whole story. But the ending does matter and sometimes we don't realize how much because we never got closure.

Endings come and go, but closure is a luxury. It often takes time, if we ever get it at all, and it rarely looks like what we think. We think closure looks like a crossed-off list, one last walk-through, a kind goodbye, meaningful words, an acknowledgment of work, love, presence, and/or contribution. We imagine a slow, thoughtful closing of the door, like the season finale of a beloved sitcom. When you get closure like that, take it and run. Even when things don't end the way you would have liked, imperfect closure is better than no closure at all. But sometimes you have to fight for it. While you imagined a tied-up ribbon, what you get is a knotted necklace. In these pages, we're not even going to try to unknot it. That's a fool's errand, and we don't have time for it. Here is where we will work to take that knotted necklace and accept it, bless it, and maybe even style it just the way it is. Because closure isn't about everything working out; it's about acknowledging the ending. How can you bring closure to an ending? Put a period on the experience by naming what you're bringing with you and what you'll leave behind.

They say when someone dies it's important to use the word "die." Not passed away, not moved on to a better place, or some other veiled attempt to avoid the *d* word. This isn't only true in death.

In his advice on writing, C. S. Lewis said that it's always best to use the plain, direct word. "Don't *implement* promises. *Keep* them."[1]

Roman Catholic priest and writer Fr. Ronald Rolheiser says we get into trouble whenever we don't name things properly.[2] With endings, especially complicated and nuanced ones, it's important to say as clearly as you are able to what has happened. With anticipated endings, this is easier to do.

She graduated.

He retired.

The job ended.

They got transferred.

I got married.

It's more difficult to use plain, straightforward language when the ending was forced or discerned, but it's important to find a few words to do so.

She cheated.

He lied.

They kicked us out.

I changed my mind.

We chose to leave.

We broke up.

She's not coming back.

Whether you're leaving or staying, plain language is key to finding a semblance of closure in an ending. Deciding to stay may be its own kind of ending, and there are things we need to let go of in this too. If we PRAY and discern in the hallway that it's time to turn around and stay put, we would do well to honor the endings that may emerge—the end of a dream we held on to, of the way things once were, the way we hoped things would be, or of relationships we miss with those who have left. This may be even more difficult for the stayers because it's not as obvious that something has ended and the grief and loss with us in the room could go unnoticed and unnamed for quite some time. As you consider what to keep with you and what to leave behind, don't count yourself out. This is for you too.

When it's time to leave a room, no matter how much preparation you've had, no matter how longed for or planned for the leaving is or was, no matter how much you begged to be let out, there will be things you can't take with you. They just won't fit through the door. Our work here is to begin to name what those things are—plainly, no mixing words, no beating around bushes.

First, you can't always take with you the kind of clarity that comes from setting the story straight. If the ending you get is one that involves systems, community, business, family, money, or love (which is almost all endings), then there's a good chance you'll have to contend with multiple perspectives, different renditions of the story, misinformed opinions, and straight-up gossip. Even if things ended reasonably well, you may still have various versions of the when, why, and how of your exit. The story is too sticky, too webbed, too large for the kind of explanations you hoped for. Versions will keep revealing themselves that you didn't even know existed. You thought the story was easy enough to tell. But there's no linear narrative that holds all the perspectives of everyone involved, and before you reach the door you realize the chatter has risen to a roar. You thought you'd found the perfect box to bring your closure with you, but what you thought was managed just pops right out: no corners, too round, extra sharp, a little pokey, and also, it's leaking. There is no box that will contain it, no bag that will cover it, no arms large enough or strong enough to carry it. The reality is, when you leave, you can only rarely take clarity with you, and you can't always leave the full story behind. You wanted closure, but you get this sideways ending instead, something hanging in the air, tears by the elevator, a bag left at your door, an unanswered text, an ending without a goodbye.

Another thing we must leave behind is regret, all of our Why-did-I's and Why-didn't-I's. *Why did I get so caught up in that conversation? Why was I compelled to tell the truth, truth, truth? Why couldn't I remain in the background and just let them think what they will? Why didn't I speak up, speak out, speak more often? Why didn't I tell them what I really thought sooner? How could I have let that go on for so long?* If you felt too weepy, too chatty, too stoic, too something other than what you imagine you should have been, this you can leave behind.

You also have to leave behind the details of the story you will never know. The details that are out there but wrong, misinformed, misled. You have to leave behind the parts that happened when you weren't in the room, the conversations they had about you and around you as the thing you once loved crumbled slowly to the ground, an emperor with no clothes dancing through the rubble. Who will tell them now that you're gone? The reality is, you don't know and that's not your job. You might have to remind yourself of this anywhere between one and one thousand times.

What else do we have to leave behind? Sometimes there is actual, nonmetaphorical stuff. When I leave a room, no matter the reason, I tend to want to hold on to notes, books, keepsakes, letters, photo albums, journal entries, clothing, and other memorabilia from my time in that room. While there's nothing wrong with keeping the stuff, the stuff's best purpose is to lead us to the sacred—specifically how the experience changed us and how it formed us. We all know the things are *not* the experience; they're the evidence that the experience was real. While it may be lovely and healing to hold on to meaningful keepsakes, consider if you have tangible things you're holding on to that could now be left behind.

Perhaps there is also a metaphorical suitcase full of things you want to work to leave behind. Could you leave behind the responsibility for everyone else's emotional well-being? Do you need to release the five-year plan that never was? Is it possible to abandon your compulsion to continue to explain yourself? Is it time to leave behind your too-small ideas of God?

When things end, it's not always clear what stays and what goes.

Like, for example, the names we carried while we occupied a room. I've been called many names throughout my life. I'm Emily P. Freeman professionally, Em to friends and family, Emmy to my mother, Bim to my college roommate, and Bird if you knew me in the early '90s. Sometimes we are named by specific traits: I am a slow processor and for years I let that name weigh me down rather than open me up. Maybe for you the unwanted name is different: impulsive, lazy, bossy, unorganized, emotional, or too sensitive. And then there are the professional names and titles we work for and earn. These names carry weight and status. Some of our names haunt us, which is why we're leaving in the first place. But other names bring us pride and joy, and we don't want to leave them behind. Teacher. Pastor. Author. Doctor. Therapist. Accountant. Journalist. Detective. Partner. Business owner. Ordained. Licensed. Certified.

Like Madeleine L'Engle wisely said, "I am still every age that I have been."[3] In the same way we bring our six-year-old self and our sixteen-year-old self to the age we currently are, we also carry every name we've ever had, whether that name was gently bestowed as a gift of love, ceremoniously given after years of hard work, or critically slung as a cruel insult, here we are, named and present, making every life decision through the lenses we've been wearing for decades, carrying them into all of our rooms. No matter if our leaving is anticipated, forced, or chosen, the names we had in the rooms we've occupied have weight and merit. Part of working for closure is recognizing those names and sometimes letting them go. Just because you discern it's time to leave something behind—a name, a box of memories, a title or position—doesn't mean it was a bad thing to have. It may have even been a good and useful thing that has served you well for a season, but now that season has passed.

The unburdening of the story, the names, the titles, and the narratives that come with the rooms we've left may bring great freedom and relief or they may cause deep sorrow and grief. Likely it will be a mix of both. How can you walk out the door when doing so means you'll also be leaving behind something that at one time seemed vital to your identity, maybe even your survival? Perhaps it feels that way still. One useful practice to cultivate closure is to also take time to name the things you're bringing with you.

When my time finally arrived and I sold my shares in the company I helped to build, I made a list of all the things I was bringing with me. It's true: my time in that room had come to an end. But many parts of that particular room were now a part of *me*. On the list, I mostly had people's names, kind and brilliant humans I had helped to hire, onboard, and work alongside. I wrote down names of the writers in our community who I never would have met if we hadn't started the company seven years earlier. I listed out many practical skills I learned while co-leading the company, like how to communicate with clarity, how to resolve conflict with a remote team, and how to teach a webinar. I got better at writing particular kinds of copy and meeting deadlines when the writing wasn't quite there. I learned how to move forward because it was time, not because I felt ready. These are skills I will have forever and will bring into all the future rooms I enter.

This overlaps with another category on my list—not only skills I had acquired but also areas where I had grown. Some questions I asked myself during this closure practice: *As a result of my time in that room, in what ways have I become more confident? How has my heart expanded because of my experience there? What did I learn that I would have had difficulty learning any other way?*

We also bring with us (and this one is less desirable but no less valuable) the knowledge of what *not* to do in the next room we enter. Because of course we know there's a lot to learn from the mentors, skilled teachers, compassionate companions, and loyal friends we meet in the rooms of our lives. As it turns out, you can also learn a lot from a person who has done it poorly. You can learn a lot about how not to be, what not to say, and what bad leadership looks like. As I walk into new rooms, I'm learning not to center myself and my own experience. This does not happen naturally but takes practice and intention. I'm learning that asking a question is often kinder than making a statement, but it only counts if you actually listen to the answer. These are things we can bring with us, the wisdom of what to avoid.

Sometimes the things we bring are not necessarily things we *want* to bring. But bring them we must. If we were hurt, if our heart was broken, if a room caused pain we cannot reverse, we'll bring the memory and we'll bring the scar. About halfway through 2021, I realized my mouth was set to a permanent frown. Was this because of age? Maybe. But also I realized that we had been wearing masks out in public, we had not been in social settings, and people outside of family hadn't seen my full face much in over a year. Quite literally I didn't have to wear the mask of persona and so my true face came out. And at that time of my life, because of the isolation, questions, and heartbreak of those years, my face was frowning. This we take with us.

But there's one thing no one can take from us, one thing we will never leave behind, one thing that is not confined to any past room, current hallway, or future room—that is the person we have become and are becoming. Hints of our next right thing can usually be found in our last right thing. I have always found this to be true. The sacred things we mark from the ending will be brought forth into our beginnings, not necessarily because of an external thing we bring with us but because of the person we have become. When things end, we come forth changed. We would do well to take some time to pay attention to those changes, to mark them, to honor them and see how they might lead us forward.

As much as I wish everything could be held, named, and either left behind or brought with us, there's a final category that might show up in endings that could keep us from experiencing closure. And that is what I call the "lost" category. It's the smoky, ungraspable, wordless, impossible to categorize absence of a thing. In every ending—happy, sad, or indifferent—something is lost. But because something is often also gained, that's what we're encouraged to focus on. We work hard to name the gifts and positive summaries of those gains. We are prone to want to count the blessings, to name the lessons, and to share all the ways our pain has been used for good. Maybe there's nothing necessarily wrong with that desire, but it can keep us from grieving what deserves grief. Something is always lost. And it's important to let the lost things be lost. Honor what you cannot name with space, compassion, and time.

It's the summer of 2017 and our family has gone to Memphis to visit John's grandmother on her birthday. She's turning 104. Since I married John, I've only known her as Budder, a nickname started decades ago by one of John's cousins who tried to say "Grandmother" and it came out "Budder." We sit with her poolside on a hot Fourth of July, and as tends to happen when we're with her, John begins to ask her a handful of questions about her life and the conversation gently leads back to God. It always does with Budder. To understand her, it's good to know a little bit of her story.

Once when we asked her what US presidents she remembered, she started thinking back. "Well, let's see. I remember President Wilson . . ." And while she rattled off a few more, I immediately had to Google the dates of Wilson's term: 1913–1921. She was born in 1913, barely a year after the *Titanic* sank and only a year before World War I began. She's always been delighted to share about her life even as she honestly doubts it's very interesting. Like the time she told us almost as an afterthought about when Elvis used to ask the football coach at the local high school if he would turn the stadium lights on at night so he and his friends could throw the football around.

"So if you drove by the stadium late at night and saw those lights on," she'd say, "you'd know Elvis was in there playing ball with his friends." Well, all right then.

That summer, if you asked someone about Budder, they would say she loves her family, she prays for each one of us by name every day, she volunteers in her community, she teaches Sunday school to first and second graders at her church, and she's happiest when she's simply in a room with those she loves. Budder is famous, if only in her own community and our family, simply by being herself.

Of course I can't possibly sum up over a hundred years of her life. I can't point you to a cool website, an impressive bio, or a slick headshot (although in her younger years she actually looked a lot like Maggie Gyllenhaal, if you ask me). As we sit there with her by the pool, we don't ask her about waiting, but evidently it's something she thinks about a lot on her own. "Every day I get such pleasure and a strengthening from a little verse that says, 'His steps are with you.' What I'm trying to make myself do is remember that little verse that says, 'Wait on the Lord.'"

As she speaks, I record some of our conversation on video, and that afternoon I share the footage on my Instagram Stories. I receive more messages from this short series of videos of Budder talking than I've ever received when I've shared stories on Instagram. I've since wondered about why that simple conversation resonated with so many of us.

She was quick-witted, remarkably present. She lived by herself, drove herself to church and the grocery store, taught Sunday school like a miracle, or a unicorn. Or both, I guess. Her husband died of a stroke when he was only fifty-four, leaving her to parent their four boys alone. Budder never remarried, living on her own for the next fifty-five years. She carried her sorrow in secret, and if she ever held grudges, she'd released them decades ago.

I look at what I know of her life, this woman who buried both a husband and later a son, John's dad. She lived through two world wars, saw the election of eighteen presidents with all of their triumphs and scandals. She lived long and she lived faithful. I think that's what people saw in her on those Instagram Stories. Yes, it's her personality, her Southern accent, and her humor. But mostly, it's her faith.

We are a generation of tired people, longing to see evidence that what we wait for in secret is worth it. We believe and yet we want help in our unbelief. Our souls make quiet work of always scanning for something consistent, something that remains even when everything changes. When we find it, the tears spill over and take us by surprise.

Down the road from Budders' is a house that over twenty million people have visited since it opened to the public: Graceland, the Memphis home of Elvis Presley. I could tell you about the mirrored staircase, the peacock stained-glass in the living room, the oddly delightful jungle room, the spotless 1970s kitchen, but since over twenty million people have visited that house, chances are you've seen all that yourself, or at least you've heard about it.

What struck me while walking through the house where Elvis lived is how in spite of all his achievements, all of his awards, money, accolades, and success, he still died in his upstairs bathroom, young, sick, and exhausted. Budder was born twenty-two years before Elvis and lived forty years past his death. His whole life fits inside hers two and a half times. But when you put aside the legend and pull back the tasseled curtain of the American dream, you'll see a man who wanted what we all want: to be loved, to be secure, and to belong. No one is immune to this. Just some of us have more money, talent, and creative ways of trying to get what we most deeply long for.

A few miles away from Graceland, Budder's small house sits on the corner in a quiet neighborhood. For years she lived there alone, praying daily for her family, living faithfully in the ways she knew how. Hers was a life of waiting. For what exactly, I don't presume to know. But I know she thought about it. I also know she brought her waiting into the presence of God.

As we talked that day by the pool in the summer of 2017, one line she shared stuck with me. Referring to her morning routine, she said, "And then the one this morning said the Lord shall take you step by step and supply all your needs. That's the first thing I do when I wake up. I turn the little light on and read that verse." As she spoke, she looked off into the distance, drew one of her hands up toward her face, and smiled. Like a little girl. A 104-year-old girl.

On the cold morning of January 12, 2018, I was on a volleyball trip as a parent chaperone when I got a call from John. "I have some sad news," he said. "Budder passed away."

The news of her death at first felt familiar, like I had imagined this moment so many times it almost felt like a memory. She hadn't been sick, but she was, after all, 104. Something in John's voice told me there was more, a heavy comma hanging in the air between us. And that's when he said it.

"There was a fire."

Instantly, I regretted my initial acceptance of her death, grabbed it back like a greedy toddler. *A fire? After all this time of living? Absolutely not. This is unacceptable.* For days after this conversation with John, I tried to reconstruct it in my mind.

How did he say it exactly? Did he say, "There was a fire?" Or did he say, "There was a house fire?" Why did he say "passed away" and not "died"? It shouldn't matter exactly how he phrased it, but it did matter, and I continued to sift through foggy memory to try to re-create the conversation.

It's painful to accept that, after 104 years of healthy and faithful living, she died in a house fire. It's confusing and sad that her life didn't have a kinder ending. I cry every time I think about it. Still, we believe Jesus was with her in her final moments and received her with tenderness and great joy. That's what we eventually came to, anyway. But in the weeks and months following her death, we grappled as a family with the unknown reality of her experience at the end.

Why did it have to end that way? There was no closure, only questions.

For anyone who is trying to come to terms with a sudden and tragic ending, it may feel like standing in a room you were content to stay in forever that either figuratively or literally burned to the ground around you. The lack of available closure can be the thing that keeps you stuck forever.

I don't have good words to offer here, but I think it's important to try to have *some* words. Too often when we're grieving, especially after a loss other people can't imagine enduring, they say they have no words. I've said it myself and have thought it a hundred more times. But one of the gifts we can give to those around us is to try to find the words, however imperfect. And one of the phrases that has helped me at an ending is declaring that the ending does not get to define the whole story. That's not to say that terrible endings are good, or that they're good for something. Terrible endings are mostly just terrible. There doesn't have to be a lesson, a reason, or a silver lining. Sometimes a cloud is just a cloud. But that terrible ending doesn't get to have the whole say.

Scripture doesn't say much about waiting for particular things, outcomes, or circumstances. Instead, we get this from Psalm 27:14: "Wait for the Lord; be strong, and let your heart take courage; wait for the Lord!" God shifts our eyes from a plan we hope for to a person we can hope in. Isn't that what God always does? Isn't that what Budder said? For her, to live was to wait. What about for us?

Here's what I know: Whatever I put at the center of the wait is what carries all the power. I can't say that I fully understand what it means to wait upon the Lord, but if God is the one inviting me into it, well then, there must be hope in that.

Here's what else I know: Budder had 104 full, complicated, beautiful years and one tragic morning that, in the truest reality, ended up being the most glorious morning of her whole long life. When things end, our heart might break, especially when the ending is unexpected, unfair, or unexplainable. The ending is a part, but it isn't the whole. Don't let the ending steal the narrative.

You are always being formed, in every beginning, middle, and end. Before rushing forward, take some time when you're ready to reflect on the path behind you.

Can you think of something in your life that ended without fanfare or acknowledgment?

Is there a ritual you can implement, a small way to put a period on an ending in a life-giving, appropriate way?

Do you need to say a formal goodbye, to have a small (or big!) celebration, or even simply to light a candle to mark a memory?

How have you grown into yourself in ways you might not have done otherwise?

What do you need to bring with you?

What are you able to leave behind?

Where have you seen God along the way?

If you're not ready to name these things, that's okay too. Just because something ended doesn't mean there was closure. Take a little time to be silent and to be still. To be watchful. To bear witness. If you can't yet see a new spark, a small shoot, or the start of a new thing, take heart. Let the lost things be lost. Ask for what you need to know. Remain open to seeing things in ways you might not expect. If nothing comes, be gentle with yourself. We don't stop living just because we're unsure. We continue on, trusting in God, as we simply do our next right thing in love.

Part 3

ON ENTERING:

How to
Walk into
a Room

What matters more than the decisions you make is the person you have become and are becoming. As you discern if it's time to stay or to leave, what does it look like to walk into rooms (whether brand-new or familiar) as the person you are now, not in spite of all the rooms you're in and have left but because of them?

We've walked around the house of our life, pointed and called out what we see. We've named who is missing and who we're becoming in the process. We've carried our questions and followed some arrows, identified the difference between peace and avoidance. We've measured our readiness, questioned the timeliness, and recognized the importance of closure when we can get it. In all of this, we've spent most of our time naming what is ending. As we enter into our final few chapters together, we'll focus on two primary questions:

What is continuing?

What is beginning?

Your answers to these questions in any given season will always inform the way you walk into a room. While the path that got you here will vary and the stories you carry and tell will be unique to you and your lived experience, when you walk into a room, you will always bring your thoughts, your feelings, and your body. There are many resources for studying and understanding these centers of intelligence, and you would do well to give these three some attention. This is not a choose-your-own adventure journey; rather it's an invitation to pay attention to all three—your mind, heart, and body—as you move through your life.

In light of what is continuing and what is beginning, ask yourself:

What do I think?

How do I feel?

What will I do next?

While we all have thoughts, feelings, and the instinct to act, we don't access all three of these centers of intelligence in equal order. One will come more naturally, one will be supportive, and one we'll have to work harder to access. Some of us feel first, others of us think first, and then there are those who act first. There are, of course, benefits and burdens to our unique way of seeing the world. The trouble comes when we think our way is wrong and someone else's way is right, or vice versa. The more I grow, the more I see how nuanced being a human truly is. Leading with one is not better than another. We all may need to rewrite the narratives we've come to believe about the burdens of our own way. Feelers are told we're too sensitive. Thinkers are told we're too cold. Doers are told we're too hasty. But walking into a room as ourselves means both owning the gift of our own way and being open to growing in a new way too. Namely, learning to integrate all three centers of our intelligence, using our acronym PRAY as a guide.

● **Point and call.**

◄ **Remember your path.**

○ **Acknowledge presence.**

➤ **Yield to the arrows.**

Walk in as a Leader

You will do what you can until you can't, and then you'll fall asleep on the chests of those who love you.

—COLE ARTHUR RILEY, *THIS HERE FLESH*

On Good Friday afternoon 2021, I sat at a single station of the cross and considered the Crucifixion of my friend Jesus. I cried alone, right there in that metal fold-up chair in an unfamiliar sanctuary at not-my church. It was several months after we had left, and though we had visited several places, we had not found a new church to call home. Sometimes weeks went by without visiting a church at all. But we are church people, we've come to admit, and the acute longing to have a place to belong and a people to belong to was always with me.

During this time, I shared the smallest bit on social media that we had left our church, mainly because I was still getting a handful of messages from kind readers moving to or visiting the area and they wanted to tell me they had visited our church and asked if we could connect. I couldn't pretend I was still there when I wasn't. But I didn't want to talk about it publicly. I wasn't ready and it wasn't time.

Meanwhile, we were finding community in unlikely places, among beautiful people with bright faces, reflecting the image of God. Some of these people were friendships preserved even after our common room was lost, including several couples who still attended the church we had left. They loved our family, and they understood why we felt we needed to go. They honored our decision to leave as we honored their conviction to stay. During that season, we remained connected with others who were asking similar questions; some of them had left their own churches but were longing for meaningful conversation around a common love for Christ. We invited them over to our house, sat in silent, distanced circles around Rembrandt's prodigal painting, shared thoughtful reflection and traded questions while staring into the shadowed reds and yellows of the art. We sat across dinner tables, reconnecting with friends from two churches ago, trading stories about parenting and friendship and how we like our pasta. We sat around front yard fires, holding space for fellow travelers, some we knew and some we didn't. We sat together, John and I, at countless morning tables, a shared grief, a shared hope, and a fractured hallelujah. What might be next? Who might we meet in this wilderness? What other fires are we being invited to sit around? What other fires are we feeling compelled to start?

Mostly I didn't have complete sentences to share about it all, about our hesitancy to trust people, about our loneliness in parenting, about our lack of answers to big and important questions. But what I did have was a heart that was breaking open in a good way. As someone who regularly shares words on the internet, I tried to extend the hope of companionship to anyone else feeling the sting of loneliness, the longing for God that held hands with deep questions and bright hope. But to do so without sharing details or betraying confidences was a most difficult task. In the midst of it all, Jesus remained uncomplicated for me. Jesus—my truest friend in the midst of an upside-down stretch of years. This is fully true. What is also fully true is that I was in a season of figuring out what God is like, testing the waters to see if the God who Jesus knows could still handle us, wondering if I should be doing more, saying more, vacillating between what I knew of love but not knowing for sure if I could trust it. And then there was also the reality of not having a church home while living in the Bible Belt.

At 11:17 a.m. one Sunday, I drove, unshowered and unkempt, to drop donations off at the Goodwill. After the better part of a year sheltering in place, zero travel, everyone home, we'd done a lot of cleaning out of closets and drawers, decluttering our house as a way of controlling at least one thing. But as a lifelong church attender, being unshowered and unrushed on a Sunday morning felt deeply strange. I didn't love it, but I didn't hate it.

Turns out the Goodwill is closed on Sundays at 11:17 a.m. Did you know? I drove back home with a car full of castoffs, feeling like a castoff myself, a growing and familiar sensation beginning to rise. It was like a recurring dream where you skip school the day of the math test, like I had an appointment I'd forgotten about, like I was here but supposed to be there. *Have I just been shamed by the Goodwill?* That day, though it felt like I was living at the end of a story, the reality was I was in the ellipsis. Yes, some things had ended, but the story wasn't over. I wouldn't be driving castoffs to the Goodwill on a Sunday morning forever. But that's what I was doing for now.

Still, I was aware of how this might look on the outside, what other people might think. Here we were, John and Emily Freeman, him having been a pastor at two local churches in the past, me an author of many faith-based books. Here we were, having just left our church of seven years, where we had led a small group and volunteered on Saturday mornings, where I had spoken at the last women's weekend retreat, where John had been on the preaching team, where we were trusted and loved among people we loved and trusted. Here we were, two people who had master's degrees, his in pastoral ministry, mine in spiritual formation. And here we were, home on a Sunday morning, no one wondering where we were, no place to fully belong. Should we have tested the ropes of the system for longer to see if they would've held? Had we acted in haste? Had we made the wrong decision?

One of the things that can keep us hesitant to change our minds, to leave formerly beloved rooms, or to confidently walk into new ones is a pervasive fear of what other people will think. They say the opposite of people-pleasing is learning not to care what people think. But that would just be another kind of wrong. I've learned I don't have to stop caring what people think. I'm learning to care in a different way. I'm learning that the opposite of people-pleasing is leadership. It's time to broaden our definition of leadership to include those spaces where we aren't in charge. It starts with leading ourselves first.

When I mention to people that John and I love to watch *Survivor* and *American Idol*, their response is usually, "Wait, what? I thought those shows went off the air years ago." Oh no, my friend. As of this writing, they are both still going strong. For twenty-two years, the unscripted reality show *Survivor* has tested the limits of human capacity, forcing people to make complex decisions and meet extreme physical demands with a limited amount of resources. It's fascinating to watch this human experiment, the lengths people will go to in order to win, the connections people make in a pressure-filled environment that they may never have made in their regular lives. As someone who pays close attention to the role our decisions play in our formation, I'm a true *Survivor* fan.

My favorite part of *American Idol* is the early weeks during auditions, when young singers show up to perform in front of the judges, hoping to get a ticket to Hollywood to continue in the competition. I still remember where I was when I watched first-time *Idol* winner Kelly Clarkson, wearing a shirt made out of pants, sing "At Last" in her 2002 audition in front of Simon Cowell, Randy Jackson, and Paula Abdul. (I called Kelly to be the winner on day one!) Back then the show had a different vibe. It seemed somewhat low-budget, was branded with lots of neon blue, and the talented singers and the not-so-talented singers received equal airtime.

That was nearly twenty years ago, and *American Idol* has evolved, redefined, and rebranded itself over the years. Now, though they still have wacky auditions, they include less of those. When they do allow a silly audition to come through, judges Luke Bryan, Lionel Richie, and Katy Perry have found a way to be playful and supportive of the person even while gently letting them know they will not be going to Hollywood.

The season 19 premiere featured the audition of a daughter of two high-profile political figures. She seemed to want to make a name for herself separate from them—at least that's how the show presented her. At sixteen, though she stood with her chin up, she couldn't hide how thin her confidence actually was, youth and insecurity tucked neatly into black leather pants. She sang her first song and I thought it was really good but the judges encouraged her to sing a second song. After removing her shoes and loosening up, her performance was even better, but she still seemed insecure. When she was finished, Katy looked at her thoughtfully and offered some sound advice. "There's a lot of noise in your life," she said. "You have to calm the storm that is around you, meaning, before you sing, you need to get off your phone. You need to stop reading your comments, push it aside, because if not, you may not ever rise above your dad or your mom. It's your choice."[1]

Like this young girl, we all have the capacity to live our lives in such a way that we forget who we are, hurrying through our minutes, looking for the next important thing, overly attentive to what people think of us, and addicted to our own press. But remember: the antidote to pleasing people is not refusing to care what they think. It's learning to care in a different way. During that Sunday morning drive home from the closed Goodwill, I was continuing the work of learning to care in a different way, though I wouldn't have named it that way at the time.

In his book *A Failure of Nerve*, Edwin Friedman writes about leadership in the age of the quick fix. He writes about the systems of families and institutions, and calls out the peacemongers—those who are highly anxious risk avoiders. He describes this kind of leader as one who is "more concerned with good feelings than with progress, someone whose life revolves around the axis of consensus, a 'middler,' someone who is . . . incapable of taking well-defined stands."[2] He submits that while these types of leaders "are often 'nice,' if not charming," they lack the ability (or rather, the willingness) to co-exist with conflict or the anxiety of others. The antidote to the peacemonger is what Friedman calls a "well-differentiated leader," which is someone who knows how to lead herself.

A well-differentiated leader has clarity about their own personal core values. They can be *separate* from others while remaining *connected* with others. They can manage their own emotional reactions and therefore are able to take stands, to speak up, and to risk displeasing. It isn't particular skills or techniques of leadership that count the most, but a leader's ability to be present and engaged even when the system (or the group) is displeased.

What Katy Perry was saying to that young contestant was essentially this: lead yourself first. Be present and be attuned. Not to the anxious, fickle system of commenters with their likes, shares, and opinions; instead, show up as yourself without permission from the anxious system.

People-pleasing is evidence of an unhealthy emotional system and is not a brush-it-away, bless-your-heart kind of bad habit. When you're stuck in a vortex of deeply caring what other people think, you're held captive in a system you're too afraid to question. People-pleasing is a serious problem and a dangerous cancer, and if you don't find the courage to name it and the clarity to reject it, the prognosis is grim. It's keeping you from your best work, your best rest, and it's sabotaging your freedom.

And here's the secret about people-pleasing no one really tells us: it doesn't actually please the people. When you're trying to please the people rather than working to discern from a centered, whole-hearted place, your work will never be enough. It will always exhaust you and never fully please those around you. Nobody wins and no one is free. What wounded, anxious people need most is not you as they think you ought to be but the solid presence of a well-differentiated leader who insists on being okay with or without their consent. This is as true for a parent as it is true for a president.

As you begin to walk into a room, whether it's a room you've entered a thousand times before or a room you're entering for the first time today, here are three ways to enter as a leader even when you're not in charge.

First, you have to know who you are. My dear friend Dr. Natasha Sistrunk Robinson is a graduate of the US Naval Academy, visionary and founder of Leadership LINKS (a leadership education organization), and a sought-after international speaker, leadership consultant, and author. In conversation with her, she said something I never forgot: "There are some places that you cannot go to find yourself, to figure out who you are. The only way you survive it is that you know who you are when you get there." If we continue to walk into rooms without knowing who we are, then we could be stuck in a cycle of looking around to figure it out rather than looking within, to our life with God, to our image bearing identity, to our truest, newest self.

Second, when you know who you are, you have to have rhythms in place to practice being who you are. What core values are vital to your well-being such that if you were to forget them or cast them aside, you would not be living an integrated life? What needs to be true about your rhythm of life so that you can show up as the person you are and not be so easily moved, swayed, or influenced to be a person you are not? What two-word mantras and breath prayers do you return to in times of confusion, disruption, fear, anger, or shame? Creating a rhythm of life that helps you rehearse being you might sound strange, but it's just a different way of naming life-giving spiritual rhythms.

Third, once you know who you are and practice being who you are, you also need to learn to make peace with crisis. I don't mean you have to live in a constant heightened state of emergency or that you need to accept the fact that trouble exists and you should not do anything about it. But your job is not always to fix everything. Friedman writes, "Living with crisis is a major part of leaders' lives. The crises come in two major varieties: (1) those that are not of their own making but are imposed on them from outside or within the system, and (2) those that are actually triggered by the leaders through doing precisely what they should be doing."[3]

The fact remains that most crises can't be simply resolved, and sometimes, when we do our next right thing, when we leave one room and enter another or stay behind when everyone else leaves, it may actually *cause* the crisis we hoped to avoid. All the more reason why we need to know who we are, be able to self-lead, and remain a fixed point to the extent that we are able. Part of this work is discerning between true peace and discomfort avoidance, as we talked about in chapter 7. It is your well-differentiated presence, not your fancy technique or your ability to please everyone, that will make the biggest difference. The sooner you realize the myth of people-pleasing, the better equipped you'll be to show up as you in the world, with confidence and peace.

Walking into a room as a leader means developing patience to follow arrows when what you really want is an answer. It means knowing the difference between peace and avoidance. It means learning how to make decisions because it's time, not because you feel ready. And it means developing the practice of waiting even when you're ready but you know it isn't time. It means knowing and naming when something has ended, developing a practice of creating the closure you need, and honoring the closure you'll never get. These are a few markers you can point to in order to know you're beginning to embrace your own unique brand of leadership in the rooms you're walking into and the rooms you've left behind.

It's January 2022. Friends and colleagues are gathered at my house, among them a man I've known for many years. In the midst of conversation, he says something I deeply disagree with, something that insults at least three people in the room and whole populations of people outside of the room. Instantly, my thoughts and feelings are activated while my body shuts down; I can feel it as it happens. I can't find my voice, can't hear what comes next. My heart is pounding. There's a whooshing sound in my ears. *Does anyone else hear it? It's so loud!* I glance at a trusted friend who is with me. She catches my eye and we both leave the room. It's the only action I know to take at the moment.

Once out of the room, the pace of my breathing picks up, shallow and floating. My eyes, wide and alert. Shame washes over me like warm butter, filling up my limbs, then sparking at the surface. Here I am, in my own house, and I can't refute him. I'm shaking now, heart pounding. *Seriously, does anyone hear it? Does anyone hear me?* Of course they don't because I'm silent. I don't say a word.

Minutes go by and a few people trickle out of the room behind me, a mirror image of me: eyes wide, heads shaking. The stench of arrogance and the pride of certainty permeate the air in my own house. I can't find my voice to stand up, to speak out, to say words to dispute him. I feel like a coward.

And so there are versions of our past selves that we are still ashamed of, that we still shame.

You should have known better.

You should have said something.

You should have defended the people you say you believe in and support.

It's true—I should have. But what is also true is I didn't. And I'm not sure I had the tools to do it then. Growth isn't always immediate, and it isn't always linear. As we grow into the person we are becoming, our actions may be the last to catch up. Yes, I cared what people thought, probably too much. Retrospect wears strength-colored glasses, fortified by time and growth and perspective. If it happened now, I hope I would show up differently. But it happened then, and I was not ready. Is there possibly leadership in this too?

In those moments, leadership meant paying attention to my thoughts, feelings, and body. Leadership meant survival, tending, and doing what I could. Now leadership looks different. Now it looks like holding compassion toward myself for not knowing what to say then or how to say it well. And it looks like extending that same compassion to others when they respond in ways I may not understand. I have more tools, more space, more grace for myself now. But that day, I wasn't ready. And being able to name that, to notice and honor it? That's leadership too.

I used to think being a good leader meant you had answers, could speak with authority, and were able to defend your decisions at every turn, including what you believed about God, the world, and just about everything else. I used to think our job as Christians was to study theology and then figure out the correct way to apply it to our everyday lives. As it turns out, this is one way to connect with God, but not the only way. And it's somewhat of a privileged perspective. What about those who are illiterate? What about communities of people who are isolated? What about those on the margins without access to the books and the scholars? Are they destined to live a less-than kind of life, one that cannot be formed into the likeness and goodness of a loving, present, dynamic God? This could not be so.

When you're working things out in your mind and have a sense *something doesn't fit here, something isn't right*, pay attention. This could be a caution flag, alerting you to an arrow that will lead to your next right thing. You may be encountering the real presence of the Divine but you haven't yet learned the theology, the study of God, that gives you language to describe it. I wish I would have known sooner that there is deeper language than words.

I am a person who loves language. I got my undergraduate degree in educational interpreting for the Deaf and became nationally certified as a sign language interpreter after graduation. Studying a language for a degree means you get to know not only the language you're learning but also your native language from which you're interpreting. You pay attention to nuance, to syntax, to the tone and timbre of spoken words and phrases so that you can accurately represent them in signed language. Though the professional room of sign language interpreting is one I left many years ago, I still respect the language and its role in Deaf culture and love watching skilled interpreters do their thing. I know some people might think interpreters are overdoing it with all the facial expressions and seemingly exaggerated movements. I know when you see them on TV you may not understand all the face pulling, the leaning forward and back in space. But what I can tell you is that in American Sign Language, a statement made with an upraised eyebrow means something completely different than that same statement delivered with the brows furrowed. Just like emphasizing certain words in English can change the meaning of a sentence, the same rules apply in American Sign Language. One hand motion may represent a fully developed idiom with history and context. One glance can communicate a whole vibe. Spoken and signed language delivers meaning, but meaning isn't delivered only through this kind of organized language.

What I'm discovering (with great delight and wonder) is that being a Christian means that I'm aware of an invitation to pay attention to my life and to how and where God is moving among us. Bonus if I can name it and find the theology that applies. It means understanding that theology cannot be divorced from humanity. It means there's often a mystery beyond what I have the ability to point and call to, or sometimes give spoken language to, but that doesn't mean it's any less real.

In her book *Leaving Church*, Barbara Brown Taylor wrote about how standing next to a spring brought these thoughts to mind. "How it worked was a complete mystery to me, but there was no denying the effect. Simply to stand near that spring was to experience living water. Later I would find the Celtic theology that went with the experience, in which God's 'big book' of creation is revered alongside God's 'little book' of sacred scripture."[4]

Brian Zahnd gives us a solid and transformative metaphor in his book *When Everything's on Fire*. He talks about theological houses, about the spaces we construct (or that are constructed around us), either on purpose or not. It's natural that anytime we say something we believe about God, something we're certain is true, we're constructing our own theological house. We do this without thinking, and while large parts of the house might be solid, sometimes the house we're constructing has dark corners, an unsure foundation, and overconfident supporting beams made of hollowed-out wood. He writes about his own experience: "After my initial encounter with Christ, I began to construct my theological house. Every time

I formed an opinion about God or dared to assert that God was a certain way, I was building my theology—even if I was almost entirely unaware of doing this. I didn't think of myself as constructing a theology. I simply thought, *these are the things that I know about God* (whether they were true or not) . . . For twenty-five years or so, my theological house was, shall we say, adequate. Or so I thought."[5]

This is, for me, a profoundly helpful metaphor. The house may work for a season of our life or faith journey. But I know what it means for the rooms of my theological house to begin to feel ever so slightly stale, the wallpaper peeling at the corners, the furniture packed in a little too tightly. This doesn't mean it was a bad house or that I was a failure at keeping it, but that a normal part of faith is to continue to grow in God. Sometimes that means some rearranging is in order. This is an ending but also a beginning.

As I listen to my own life and pay attention to the rooms I'm entering, I keep waiting to find the exact right theological room to belong to. While the rootedness of my faith remains the same, the way I talk about it has shifted. While my eyes are trained steadfastly on my friend Jesus, my hands open to God, my heart receptive to Spirit, I'll admit my mouth is shut more often than it used to be when it comes to my faith, a waiting listener in the presence of the Divine. I'm looking into faces, leaning into conversations, trying on creeds. I'm listening for resonance, watching for reactions that look like Jesus. I've got my ear to the ground, to the grate, to the wall with a glass, cupping my hands around my ears, shushing the chatter in my own head, listening for familiar phrases, credible indictments, searching for proof that I definitely do not belong or that I definitely do. What if this theological curiosity is its own room, of sorts? What if it's not a room at all but a gathering without walls? It's the fire in the forest, beyond the tracks of the train. My need, desire, obsession with finding the "right" room keeps me from engagement, from connection, from who God is right now. When I'm busy looking for ways to define God, I'm not able to experience God. This is continuing. This is a beginning.

In your own areas of influence, I wonder what it would look like to quiet the noise in your life, to calm the storm that's around you (at least for a few moments), and to move into your next right thing as the person you are and not the person you think you ought to be. Owning the choices I've made as I've navigated the various rooms of my life is one way I'm practicing the art of leadership.

Lead yourself first. Quiet the noise. Clear the clutter. Silence the shame. And then? Consider that your next right thing might be disruptive, bring discomfort, or reveal a difficult truth. People-pleasing is keeping you from your greatest contribution, your brave yes, your strong no. What people need most are your solid presence and your steadfast insistence on being okay with or without their consent. We don't need you to please us. We need you to lead us. But first you have to lead yourself.

11

Walk in as a Listener

Curiosity lights our way to compassion.

—SHANNAN MARTIN, *START WITH HELLO*

I pull in after dark, the parking lot of the church nearly full. I'm glad to see the front entrance is obvious, as I've never been to this church before, even though we have dear friends who are regular attendees. I'm not late to the evening ordination service, but I'm one of the last ones in, so I grab a seat near the back and place my bag on the empty chair next to me. Unsure what to do with my hands, I pick up my bag again and put it on the floor at my feet instead. As we wait for the service to start, I lean back down, dig around in the bag, and grab my phone, mindlessly clicking apps as if I have something important to look at. A few people sit alone behind me, but most seem to be with family or friends, engaged in the kind of casual conversation that happens before a service begins.

This month marks one full year since we wrote the letter to the leaders of our former church, one year since we've officially been churchless. John and I have visited two or three other churches in town with varying degrees of regularity, but tonight I'm here by myself to celebrate one of my dearest friends as she is ordained as a deacon into the Anglican Church. While I miss the days when she worked as an event planner and traveled with me to speaking events, now Melissa is working full time as the youth pastor at her church and has met all the requirements to become a member of the diaconate. Back in 2013 she was the one beside me at that conference in Austin, supporting my work. Nine years later, I'm here with others to bear witness to and affirm her ordination.

When I finally get still, I notice the dark smoky spice of incense hanging in the air around me, and I realize tears have emerged, surprising my face. Without thinking, without conscious memory, a familiar invitation presents itself unbidden in my mind:

Come, all you who are tired and travel-stained, footsore and famished; Come with your fellow travelers to find companionship and comfort. For here Jesus—who knows what it is to wander, watch, and wrestle in desert places—waits to meet us here and welcome us in, offering rest and renewal, solace and strength, for the journey still to come.

What are these tears doing here, holding hands with this familiar blessing? Why have they arrived now, before the service has even started? As a person who feels her way through the world, I'm familiar with emotion that shows up without explanation. My feelings are not my only source of information, but they are always first. I may not fully understand why I feel a particular way, but I am nearly always able to name the emotion I feel. While the question of *why* is usually unhelpful, this time I don't have to wonder for long before I have my answer. I realize it's because this room smells exactly like the chapel at the Catholic retreat center in Kansas where I've spent many transformative weeks over the past five years. And this blessing that comes to my mind is one we read each time we arrive there.

Most of us don't like to cry in public, especially among strangers. But in a room full of people, it's not actually the tears that draw the attention. It's when you lift your hand to wipe them away—that's what people notice. Refusing to address them means you'll blend right in, so in this moment as the service begins, I stand completely still, singing along to the familiar chorus, cheeks and neck wet with the evidence, one tear traveling all the way down to my bra.

When I walked into this room here in my hometown of Greensboro, North Carolina, I was still travel-stained, footsore and famished: for the fellowship of friends, for the communal connection with God, for belonging. As John and I visit other churches, filled with kind people and mostly familiar liturgies, we aren't in a hurry and we're still sorting through what it means for us to hold a high Christology, to be Trinitarian in our theology, contemplative in our practice, and generous in our orthodoxy. We aren't fool enough to think we'll find a perfect church, but we want to find one where our whole family is welcome into fellowship without caveat or agenda, and where we know your whole family is welcome too.

After a beautiful ceremony, packed with meaning, ritual, and affirmation, I linger in the back of the sanctuary and watch as Melissa makes her way to her waiting friends and family seated near the front. After a minute or two, I join them there, greet her children, whom I've watched grow up, hug her husband, whom I've known since college. When I reach her, we instantly laugh and cry, as this has become our new greeting. I love her deeply and am so proud of the person who she is and is becoming. As we embrace, circling up twenty-five years of shared history, she simply says how glad she is to know I've come. The crowd around us is moving from the sanctuary to an adjacent room for a reception, and we turn to face that direction. It's slow work, as she continues to be stopped by congregants bearing cards, gifts, and words of affirmation.

I don't know many people in the room, so I mainly observe the evening as it carries on, the celebratory nature of it, the laughter and chatter that fills the space, the way the light is reflected in windows-turned-mirrors, a warm contrast to the dark February night. And I'm glad to be a listener here, to bear witness to it all, to see the fruit of her investment in this community. It's all evidence of time, deep roots, and strong connections.

After a while of mingling and meeting new people, I say my goodbyes and head to my car. Seated behind the wheel, I notice a rush of emotion. Once upon a time my family were the ones in a room filled with people, surrounded by warm affirmation, community, and support. *We had that once too. We were known once too.* As I start the car and make my way home, envy works to find a space in me. But it doesn't sit down. Instead, I intentionally bring my thoughts to the fore in order to name what I think and feel, and intentionally choose what I will do in response. This movement isn't always so obvious and intentional, but tonight it is, and I pay attention to the arrow. I can name that while I feel a little sad, I'm also soft and hesitantly hopeful. For now, I also feel gratitude. This is a new exchange for me. Learning how to walk into a room like a leader means listening to my feelings, honoring when they show up, and leading myself through them first. It also means listening to my thoughts, not only the ones that seem acceptable and nice but also the ones that point out what I've lost, what I miss, and what I wish were true.

This night had great potential to derail me, to send me spiraling into loneliness, jealousy, or regret over the rooms we left and what we left behind. But this was not my experience tonight. Melissa and her family put down roots in this faith community, and those roots have sprouted shoots, leaves, and blooms. It's a room they are committed to, one they've stayed in, for now. It's been the right choice for them, and it's good for me to celebrate their choices even while we've made different ones, ones that I'm still grieving. Our lives are quieter now and we aren't as busy as we used to be. But I'm finding trusted voices in the wilderness. And I don't feel so lonely anymore.

Listening to all three centers of our intelligence takes courage. We may fear we won't have what it takes to deal with what we might hear. I've given my whole vocational life to the work of listening, first as a sign language interpreter and now as a spiritual director. I'm convinced it's one of the most transformative practices we can engage in. We often don't prioritize listening, though, because it seems passive, it seeks no attention, and it doesn't satisfy our compulsion to achieve, produce, or solve. Listening can be deeply inefficient, counterintuitive to our expertise, and insulting to our bottom line.

Discernment is a way of listening that integrates the movement of God, our deeply held desires, and our connection to the world around us. This means we have to find a way to access our feelings without dismissing, repressing, preaching to, or shaming ourselves for them. To walk into a room as a listener means we're listening not only to the room around us but also to the room within, the interior home we bring with us, the shelter of our inner life. The work is not just attunement but also the effort it takes to allow what is to rise to the surface without threat of judgment, to avoid filtering out the stuff we hear that we don't like. When we enter rooms as a listener, what are we listening to and what are we listening for?

When I graduated from college, I got my first official job as a sign language interpreter at a local public high school and was assigned to one student at one school for the duration of the year. As interpreters, we're proficient in both receptive and expressive skills, responsible for both accurately communicating the teacher's lectures and, in turn, accurately voicing a student's signed expressions and responses. Everything that happens in a school has to be accessible to every student. I interpreted everything: geometry, algebra, history, PE, pep rallies, field trips, non-captioned videos, basketball games and practices, locker room huddles, morning announcements, and even some high school friend drama. Outside of the classroom, during my short stint as a community interpreter, I interpreted counseling sessions, symposiums, ceremonies, doctor appointments, assemblies, community plays, and more. I may not be working as a sign language interpreter anymore, but being trained in the field of listening, language, and intercultural mediation required skills I use on a daily basis now, as a writer, as a spiritual director, and just as a person. My most poignant memory of what it means to listen to the room was during my years as an interpreter at a local university.

I was scheduled to interpret for an awards luncheon, and the room was filled with a mix of scholarship donors, faculty, staff, and students. At least one Deaf student was among those being honored that day. Upon entering the banquet hall, I found the table where the student I was assigned to interpret for would be seated, but the trouble was the organizers had set me a plate as well, like I was one of the guests. I was a new interpreter at the time, really wanting to follow the letter of the law. And the rules said that I was there to work, not to participate. Technically it wasn't appropriate for me to eat lunch at the table, as if I were a part of the event. But practically I needed to be seated in such a way that the student could see me but also I could hear the conversation around the table and voice for the student loudly enough so the other participants at the table could hear. This is complicated while attempting to interpret over a meal, but I worked to do my best and remain professional.

When the server came around with the salad, I politely declined. The people around the table encouraged me to eat, passing me bread and butter. I declined again, having to repeat myself for several different courses, all the way to dessert. Instead of helping me to blend into the background, my constant decline of the food ended up bringing more attention to me than would've come if I would've just simply let them serve me food and left it there untouched.

Here's what I missed: Our dining companions were not accustomed to having an interpreter at their table, and there wasn't time for the student to prepare them in advance for how to work with an interpreter. This may have been some of their first exposure to sign language, Deaf culture, or the interpreting process. I had underestimated how uncomfortable these participants, many of them older, would feel having someone seated at their table who wasn't eating. My lack of experience at the time had me relying solely on the rules rather than on my intuition and reading what the moment required.

This luncheon comes to mind for me a lot, particularly in group settings where I'm tasked with leading or facilitating a conversation in a listening practice. Because there's *the practice* and then there's *the room*. If I hold too tightly to my planned agenda, I will almost always miss an opportunity to attend to what's happening in the room. Does it feel risky to hold my own agenda loosely? Yes, absolutely. But I never regret scrapping an agenda to attend to a nuanced human moment that might otherwise have gone unnoticed or unnamed. Good listeners read the room, both the literal room we're in and the invisible room of our own internal experience that can show itself through our feelings, our thoughts, and our body.

Listening to my body is not something I'm great at. Some days I desperately wish I were an expert in everything. I want to know brain science, psychology, and the astronomical phases of the night. I want to be an expert on religion, home decor, and the history of the church. As it is, I know a little bit about a lot of things (though I'm working to become a specialist in a few). But one little bit I know for sure is that my body is always speaking. And I also know that I've spent a lot of my life ignoring, discounting, and dismissing what she says.

What I don't always know (and wish I were more expert at) is what she's saying, why she's saying it, and what to do about it. For example, there were a few days recently when my legs were swollen. Not excessively. (I bore twins in my body so I understand excessive swelling. This was not that.) But it was just a weird thing that doesn't ever happen to me. My first instinct was to be annoyed and to seek an answer. My second instinct was to Google it. Of course I found many common and concerning causes for swollen legs, but in the end I just ate less salt, drank more water, and got more sleep. All is now well. So what was my body telling me? I think it was simply: *Pay attention to me.* We see this when we have a cold or the flu and our body feels worn down and tired. Our body is signaling: *You are not well. It's time to rest.* We can push through that, or we can pay attention and do something to attend to our well-being.

When a small child acts out, sometimes we'll hear a parent say, "Oh, ignore her. She's just trying to get attention." I've probably said this before too, when my kids were small. But withholding attention is a form of neglect, and we do it with our bodies all the time. I'm learning to pay attention, to slow down, to be kind and compassionate toward my actual flesh and bones. To listen to my body like I would to a friend. This is easier said than done.

As you begin to experience life after either leaving particular rooms or deciding to stay even when conditions are less than ideal, you may begin to realize all the ways you have had to disconnect from your body in order to be accepted, to belong, or to survive. Listening to your body has not always been a safe or welcome practice.

It might feel unnatural, indulgent, selfish, or even dangerous to pay attention to the experience of your body in a room. But in order to show all the way up for your life, in order to know if the rooms you're in are the rooms where you're meant to stay, in order to contribute your good and beautiful gifts to influence rooms toward equity, justice, peace, and inclusion for everyone in the kingdom of God, it's imperative that you become a fully integrated person. And you cannot do that by ignoring the language your body speaks.

Our lives tell a story our bodies won't let us forget, and learning to discern how Spirit speaks to us by engaging our actual senses has the potential for a wholehearted confidence to grow with us into every room we enter. Because while I fully believe in the gifts of being a feeler and a thinker, I also want to spend some time with the spiritual practice of paying attention to my senses, of not valuing the invisible more than the visible, of remembering Jesus came as a human person to Earth even though he was fully God in heaven. What does it mean for us that he had a nose, two eyes, and a mouth? Jesus with brown skin and fingernails matters for every room I enter. God who rested, laughed, cried, spit, and bathed is a God with bodily senses.

In her book *Embracing the Body*, author Tara Owens submits that our bodies teach us about God. "It is only in our bodies that we experience God at all; without them, we cease to exist. When we focus only on our 'spiritual lives'—the interior realm of thought and feeling—we lack foundational understanding and attentiveness to that which is at the center of our very lives, the only vehicle through which God reaches us and we reach others: our incarnate, bound-in-time, utterly beloved bodies."[1]

As we enter physical and metaphorical rooms, here are some questions to carry to help you to pay kind attention to your experience as a body:

What do I see? When you enter a room, look around and take note of who is there and who is missing. Pay attention to the light and the shadows, the seating and the doors. This is a practice of observation, not one of judgment.

What do I hear? Who does the most talking, and what do they say? What sounds distracting? What sounds like home? What does love, joy, peace, and patience sound like to you? Do you sense these qualities in the room?

What do I smell? Is it earthy, antiseptic, natural, or clean? Is it familiar, repugnant, or stale? What memories are evoked from the smells in this room? What smells curious? What smells like comfort?

What feelings are emerging? What is the atmosphere like in this room you just entered? Is the air warm or cool? Do you want to open or close? Do you notice comfort or discomfort in your body or in the space around you? Are you aware of welcome or rejection? How do you know? What signals is your body giving you that you are anxious, welcome, free, ignored, or relaxed?

Listening to our bodies tells us a story, even if it's not the whole story. If you walk into a room and feel immediately anxious, self-conscious, or uncomfortable, here is a yellow flag. Rather than immediately running out the door, consider your body first. What do you see, hear, smell, and feel? What are the signs and signals? This can slow you down long enough for your mind and heart to catch up to your body. As we learned from Dr. Hillary L. McBride in chapter 7, don't confuse the initial emotional and bodily responses as signals that something is wrong and you need to leave. They could mean that, but they don't automatically mean that. We can acknowledge discomfort without labeling it as an arrow to danger.

And so we're listening to our feelings, to the room, and to our bodies. As we do, we'll notice how the process of leaving rooms and entering new ones can be disorienting at best, devastating at worst. Maybe you no longer recognize your surroundings or yourself. New struggles may emerge in this process, new insecurities or questions. How can we remain open to a new room when we know how difficult it may one day be to leave? Like roots in the ground or weeds in a garden, growth takes turns we don't know how to plan for, but it may also yield blooms we didn't dream to expect. When a plant grows, it goes through necessary change, but it never goes back to a seed. It becomes something new. Maybe there's no normal to get back to. Maybe there's only you, doing the next right thing you know to do, and releasing yourself from the hallway.

Consider how you've typically measured the decisions you make. Do you measure their merit based on how you feel while you're making them? How others respond to them? Are they made in freedom, peace, and love? Do you call something good if it yields productive results and bad if it flops? What is success and what is failure, and who gets to say which is which? Those are important questions to consider. The metrics by which you measure a good decision may need to be recalibrated depending on if you're entering a room for the first time or wanting to adjust the way you've entered the same room in the past.

What's even more important than the decisions you make is the person you're becoming while you make them. The less confident you feel about your decisions, the more you tense up, clench your jaw, lose sleep, and scold yourself for being too much of something bad and not enough of something good. When this happens, it's more likely you'll be unkind to yourself. What if you practiced doing the opposite? If you find yourself feeling stuck, instead of holding your breath, try letting it out. Instead of scolding yourself, try speaking words of comfort out loud. Even if you don't fully believe them right now, speak them in faith as a hopeful practice, a way of professing something true even if it doesn't feel true yet.

When listening to others, what if we were the kind of listeners who take off our shoes in reverence when they trust us with their stories, their fears, and disappointments? What if we swiftly and fiercely refused to try to fix, one-up, rescue, entertain, poke fun, scold, or compete? What if we stopped trying to fill the quiet spaces with so many words? And what if we did this not only for each other but also for ourselves, like our very own friend? I've spent more time in silence in the last two years than perhaps in the last decade combined, and I'm exhausted from the work of it even though embracing silence fits well with my particular spiritual personality. I'm grateful for the ways the silence surrounds, sits with, comforts, and forms me. Silence is alive. Listening is how we embody the energy of it. But getting quiet and thoughtful may not be your most natural way of listening to yourself. It's one way, but it's not the only way. Knowing and naming your own spiritual personality can serve as an arrow to how best to listen to yourself well in the kind presence of God.

The first time I enter the meetinghouse, I feel like I have come home. The room is filled with light this morning, sunbeams bathing the wooden pews by the windows in this space where these mostly lifelong Quakers meet. When something resonates like that, my instinct is to baptize the moment in permanence, claim it as my own, fully immerse myself. I want to find a period for this ongoing paragraph so I can wrap up the ellipsis and close this never-ending chapter. But if the process of discernment has taught me anything, it's that there is almost always no *once and for all*. There's only *for now*. As much as I sometimes yearn for the certainty of roots, I'm beginning to rest in the truth that roots are something we can take with us wherever we go, and that is good and beautiful in its own way.

The room is filled with people whose faith is deeply rooted in listening. It's such a high communal core value here that in the semi-programmed meeting we've recently been attending, they even have listening instructions on small cards stuck in the backs of the pews. These instructions are meant to be helpful for anyone who may be unfamiliar with the held silence of a Quaker meeting, making a clear distinction between listening and speaking.

Quakers are deeply comfortable with held silence, and at this particular meeting, their gathering time is simple, beginning with some music, a reading, and a prayer. Their commitment to equality, peace, simplicity, and truth is evident in their order of service. The pastor brings a short message from scripture and then welcomes everyone to enter into silence, what they call "waiting worship." Congregants are all invited into a time of listening, encouraged to speak only if Spirit leads them to do so and then to listen well when others speak. After a few moments in silence, someone will stand in response to the message. Another person shares a thought they had during the silence or a poem or passage of scripture that was meaningful to them. This is how it usually goes: a long-held silence, one or two people briefly speak, more silence, and then we close. One time a woman broke the silence with a simple, haunting verse of "His Eye Is on the Sparrow" with no further commentary, and I wept from the back row without moving a single muscle. Other times no one says a word and we sit in silence for a full twenty minutes until someone closes the time with a simple, rhetorical question: "Are all hearts and minds clear?"

The room is bright, unpretentious, non-performative, and holds a spirit of open kindness. There is a profound lack of hurry; even the rays of light through the windows seem slow. During our first several Sundays with the Quakers in the spring of 2022, I would recall the scene from *Fleabag* where Phoebe Waller-Bridge's character has her feminist revelation in a quiet meetinghouse, and this memory distracts me for exactly half of the waiting worship time. But as the weeks go by, that image faded and was replaced by an obsession with measuring the silence. I would look at my watch when the silence began and jot down the time in my journal:

11:32 A.M.

When the first person stood to speak (if anyone did at all),
I would record the time again.

11:43 A.M.

We were silent for a full eleven minutes.

I made a note of how long each person spoke. And then when
the next person stood to speak, I would record the time between
the speakers.

11:49 A.M.

As it turns out, measuring is not listening.

Control will always find a way.

After visiting for six months, I shared during waiting worship. I
tried to push the idea aside but then reconsidered when it persisted.
I decided I'd rather avoid the rush of adrenaline that Spirit often
brings when the arrows point to action, but I'm slow to move. I
stood, and the morning host brought the microphone to me, wait-
ing while I put on my reading glasses and balanced my journal in
my left hand. I read a blessing by Peter Greig that I had written
down months before that came to mind during the message. I read
it slowly and thoughtfully from the second to last pew from the
back. I was glad no one turned around. The Quakers don't need to
look in order to listen.

We found our quiet place among the Quakers that summer and
stayed into the fall, the silence in the waiting worship after the ser-

mon holding us, the small community sharing pink lemonade at the rise of service beneath the magnolia tree. It's the right place for our family for now, welcoming and kind, though we've kept our distance, mostly. We haven't got involved much. But it still counts as a home if you want it to, even if it's not forever. Our hearts and minds are clear as we bear witness to the work of healing that is in motion as we place ourselves in the Light. At the time of this writing, it has now been a full year since our first visit to the meetinghouse. We are still participating in worship with the friendly Quakers, and I'm not sure how long we'll stay. But we believe there's good reason Jesus left behind a community and invited us to gather with one another. And so we'll continue to do the good and beautiful work of finding our people right where we are, even if it takes some time.

When we gather in community, there's always potential for pain, for miscommunication, and differences of opinion, experience, and theological interpretation. But there is also great potential for love, for communion, and for spiritual connection. Even so, I know not all homes are permanent. Neither is every room. Maybe most of them aren't. We get disoriented when we expect the places where we have a taste of belonging to last forever. When they change, we think we've been lost or left. We think we've done something wrong. We fail to consider that perhaps this home was home for a moment, shelter from a gathering storm, respite from the torrential rains of disappointment, a place to heal for a moment in time even if it's not forever.

12

Walk in as Your Own Friend

Oprah: What's a question you think every woman should ask herself?

Quinta Brunson: Do I like myself? Do I really like myself when I'm in a room by myself, when I'm with myself, do I like who I am?

July 19, 2019, marked fifty years since *Apollo 11* made the historic trip to the surface of the moon. History highlights that moonwalk, but we would be telling a different story if the astronauts had not returned home safely. I've watched many rocket launches on TV, and the coverage is usually hours long leading up to the launch, always with a chance liftoff will be delayed because of the weather. Sometimes we'll also hear commands and conversations from mission control or from the astronauts themselves. If conditions are fair, eventually we'll get a countdown to liftoff, sometimes a timer in the corner of a screen. And the camera will follow the rocket from the smoky, fiery liftoff all the way up, shakily zooming in to capture the capsule through the lens, all heads tilted up. It's exciting to watch a rocket launch, but how many times have you watched a reentry? It may not be for lack of interest but more for lack of coverage. A capsule floating back to Earth landing somewhere in the sea doesn't get the same airtime as a smoky, fiery atmospheric exit. For all the emphasis put on missions to space and what happens once they get there, those missions would be incomplete without a solid plan to get them safely home.

There are two main types of atmospheric reentry: controlled and uncontrolled. Space debris hurling through the atmosphere is a type of uncontrolled atmospheric reentry, much like a ravaging, uncontrolled fire. A spacecraft coming home on a preplanned path is a controlled entry, like a prescribed burn. But just because it's planned doesn't mean they have agency over every part. Like divers coming up to the surface from the depths of the ocean or climbers coming down from the heights of the mountains, these reentry journeys happen in phases. Coming back is not one swift movement. There are intervals and pauses to consider, and all of that takes time and patience. Experienced travelers understand that at any point something unexpected could happen or go wrong.

Reentry has a lot of implications on the body of an astronaut, the first transition happening between space and Earth's atmosphere. A controlled reentry has three movements: entry, descent, and landing (EDL). This is all about dissipating the energy to ensure a smoother landing by using rockets, balloons, air compressors, and parachutes. But even with these safety devices and advanced technology in place, landing on Earth from space in a capsule is described

205 ▶

as feeling like a series of car crashes for the astronauts inside. With the amount of heat the command module has to endure, it's no wonder. For example, when *Apollo 11* returned to Earth in 1969, "the temperature on the CM's [command module's] surface climbed up to 5,000 degrees Fahrenheit, but the heat shields protected the inner structure of the CM. . . . From the ground, it would look as if the CM had caught on fire during its descent. In reality, the ablative covering is what kept the astronauts inside the CM safe—the material diverted heat away as it vaporized."[1]

They say when astronauts return to Earth after being in space even for just a few weeks, they feel about five times heavier than they expect to when they walk around. The longer they're in space, the greater the impact on their bodies when they return. In 1969, when Neil Armstrong, Buzz Aldrin, and Michael Collins landed on Earth after their historic lunar mission, they had to wear isolation suits as a precautionary measure in case they brought microbes back from the moon. They were even sprayed with disinfectant. (I like to imagine President Nixon himself spraying them down with Lysol.) They had to stay in isolation for a full three weeks before they were reunited with their families. More recently, when astronaut Scott Kelly returned to Earth after a year in orbit, he reported that his feet still hurt two months after being back in gravity. Just because reentry is difficult doesn't mean they're doing it wrong. On the contrary, that bumpy, fiery ride is not a mistake; it's the actual way home.

Sometimes leaving a room feels like lighting a match. And we wonder: Is this the flame of a controlled burn, like a ritual candle or a celebratory firework? Or is this the raging fire of an uncontrolled burn, one that takes everyone by surprise, seeming to ruin every-thing in its path? If leaving a room is like lighting a match, entering a room can feel like atmospheric reentry: wild, terrifying, and end-lessly unpredictable. Even when walking into a room looks normal and nondescript on the outside, it can feel wildly disorienting on the inside. But just because your entry feels chaotic doesn't mean you've entered the wrong room. It could just mean you're learning to enter a room differently now, fully aware and awake, acknowledging what you've lost, aware of the potential to get hurt again, holding compas-sion toward your thoughts, feelings, and intuition.

We can enter rooms with a gently integrated intelligence, access-ing our thoughts, feelings, and bodily experience as a leader, as a person, as a heart. We may not be in control, but we will be more *whole*. My hope is the framework and practices in this book will serve as the rockets and parachutes for your own reentry, your own entrance into a room. It won't guarantee a smooth arrival, but pointing and calling, remembering your path, acknowledging pres-ence, and yielding to the arrows you discern in hallways will con-tinue to build within you a practice of embracing all three centers of your intelligence. They will be your supportive companions as you engage in the healthy, human rhythm of leaving rooms and finding new ones.

When we discern it's time to walk out of a room, especially if it was a difficult decision, we only know what we're leaving. We don't know what's waiting in the next room. I'm learning that, in some way, something new is always waiting. It may not be what we expect, thought, or even hoped for.

But it will not be nothing.

When we exit rooms, we may say, or hear others say, that it's important to finish well, to finish strong, to complete our assignment. I'm a fan of finishing well, but I think it's important that we define our terms. What does it mean to finish well? And who gets to say?

Depending on the room and our physical, emotional, or spiritual state as a result of either being in that room or experiencing the exit from that room (Was it forced? Expected? Planned for? Discerned?), finishing well might simply mean *finishing period*. Leaving well may have as much to do with walking into a room as it does with walking out.

Much like atmospheric reentry, your entrance into your next room will almost always be accompanied by some degree of unpredictability. If you left a room in a dramatic or hurtful way, if there was a big breakup, a death, a heartbreak, or a division, chances are your exit may have felt heavy and exhausting. Walking into your next room might mean finding the courage to do just one regular next right thing: a widow going to the grocery store alone for the first time after losing her partner; a teacher entering the classroom again after moving to a new city; a retiree waking up on Monday morning three days after his retirement party; a new parent returning to work after their parental leave is over.

These milestone entries may look nondescript on the outside, which can make them easy to overlook. There won't be a medal for them—no reward, cheering crowd, or prize money. There is no welcome party or commencement ceremony for these new beginnings. They will be mostly quiet, unassuming, and private. But just because atmospheric reentry is planned and expected doesn't mean it's uneventful or smooth. The "series of car crashes" doesn't mean something is wrong. It might even mean you're on the way home.

Part of finishing or ending well after leaving a room is walking into the next room as a more fully integrated human no matter what kind of entry it is. The simplest way I can think of to embody that concept is to walk into a room as your own friend.

In the same way you asked yourself The Ten Questions about the rooms you were considering leaving, here are a few final questions to ask yourself about the rooms you are entering: ten simple ways to companion yourself across thresholds, ten questions to ask as you walk into a room.

What is mine to do? A borrowed question from Suzanne Stabile, and our answer may not come swiftly. But keeping it in mind as we walk into a room could protect us from potentially overfunctioning or trying to live someone else's life.

Where (or with whom) can I safely feel my feelings? Depending on the room, crossing a threshold can bring up a lot of emotion. Feelings don't need to be fixed; they need to be felt. While it may not be appropriate to share your feelings in every room, it's good to know and name people with whom you feel safe to do so when the time is right. And then consider if your feelings might be carrying an arrow to follow.

Who is with me? A practice of presence and awareness is a good one to embody. As you enter a room, consider who you bring along: the people who have loved you, the ancestors you have never met, the God who sees you. We never have to walk into rooms alone.

What do I need more of right now? There's no use faking it or making it sound good. Just an honest account of what you need more of: clarity, time, belonging, understanding, rest. We don't need to find the energy to try to make our needs sound impressive.

What is the best thing that could happen here? Our default could be the opposite, to ask what is the worst that could happen in the rooms we inhabit. But making a practice to also consider the best things that could happen in every room we enter allows us to move beneath the banner of a hopeful vision rather than the burden of potential catastrophe.

What have I had too much of lately? This question alone could help us to set boundaries in the rooms of our lives and to clarify if a particular room is good for us today.

What bothers me most? Many things may bother you, but maybe one bothers you *the most*. This is one to pay attention to. You can't take action in everything. But you can take action in something. What bothers you *the most* could be your first clue to your next right thing.

What do I have to offer? Your presence matters here, and we need what you have to offer in the form of the person who you are, not just what you can do for us. Knowing and naming what you have to offer—wisdom, resolve, clarity, joy, discernment, humor—is a gift to everyone in the room. And doing so from an awareness and acceptance of your own spiritual personality and personal core values will allow your offering to be uniquely yours.

What needs undoing? When faced with confusion, tragedy, chaos, or difficulty, often our first question is: *What can I do?* Consider also what might first need to be undone.

Who can I ask for help? Longevity in the work of love, activism, and ministry requires help. And so does being a person. Let's be human together.

May naming give shape to what once felt formless. And in the form, however faint, may you know you are not alone.

How we walk into a room will always carry evidence of our formation. And so decision-making and discernment are not things to be systemized, oversimplified, generalized, or delegated. But it's the actual road upon which I'm invited to walk in order to be formed more fully into the likeness of Christ. Because the discernment process is not, in fact, about simply going into a situation with a question and coming out with a clear answer. It is actually a formation process necessary to grow our faith, to teach us how to discern God's voice, and to draw us into community. Remember Iris Murdoch's words: "At crucial moments of choice most of the business of choosing is already over." The habits in my life, the way I spend my time, the things I choose to focus on, can shape me in such a way that my instinctive choice is love, joy, peace, patience, kindness, goodness, faithfulness, gentleness, and self-control. The rhythms of our lives will always influence our decisions, for better or for worse.

I am someone who believes in a God who is deeply interested and invested in our lives; not God as we wish God to be or God as we are afraid God is or a bigger and more omniscient version of our parents or our pastor or our priest but God as God actually is. My desire for us to know God together is not for the sake of knowing exactly what to do or choosing the right thing over the wrong thing or having the correct belief. But for the sake of knowing you are seen and loved, that you are not alone, that there is peace available, and you are not forgotten. Full stop. The end. No disclaimers.

Here's what that could look like as you walk into a room:

Be kind. You've survived a lot. You've even thrived, sometimes. Look at you, being human and resilient and alive! These are things to celebrate. What has your resilience cost you? What have you lived through? Maybe the thing you need to remember is that you have good instincts. That you can trust yourself. And that some things are good enough for now. So be kind to yourself and make room for kindness to others. They're surviving a lot too.

Be growing. Another parking lot comes to mind, this one outside the local coffee shop where I write. They're building a grocery store, and demolition started weeks ago. You can see where the new building will be, but there isn't much there yet except construction equipment, piles of debris, and mounds of dirt. It's a parking lot on a threshold, on its way to becoming a shopping center. What was is no longer and what will be isn't quite yet. Walking to my car after leaving the coffee shop, I notice some of those mounds of dirt in the construction zone have grass and other plants growing out of them. This parking lot is in the midst of a transition and grass is growing where it has no business. Even though the dirt isn't there for keeps, it's there for now. Seed takes root, burrows into the darkness, and shoots up to the light because that's what seeds do. They take root and grow even though things won't be this way for always, even though all is about to change, even though all seems unsettled, unsure, and unstable. The one thing change doesn't change is growth. I may avoid, resent, or fear the change, but I never regret the growth. Real growth can sometimes feel like shrinking, like smallness, like death. They don't teach you that in school.

Growing as a parent means I have less direct influence than I used to.

Growing as a business owner means I'm delegating my roles to the next generation of leaders.

Growing as a writer means sometimes my work is hidden, unread, and private.

Growing in my faith means my list of certainties has shrunk.

Growth is good, but it may not present as taller, louder, bigger, or noticeable.

Some of the deepest growth that has happened in my life looks shorter, quieter, smaller, and hidden.

If you want to walk into a room as your own friend, be someone who is growing. Just make sure to define your terms.

Be you. When hints of your own design scare you, one choice you might make is to run. I've done it over and over again. I've stayed silent when I've known I am meant to speak out. I've stayed still even when I felt compelled to move. When hints of my own potential show up in me, I haven't always welcomed it. But I'm starting to. And it feels like waking up. I hope we can all benefit from this reminder to pay attention to our own voice, to how God might want to move within and around us.

What if you could trust yourself? Really and truly? Not to the exclusion of everything and everyone else. Not you and you alone, like a rock or an island. But what if you could actually trust that God has given you a mind, a heart, and a body that are capable of following arrows, making sound choices, and discerning wise next steps? I don't mean to imply that there is any less blessing, giftedness, leadership, or strength in the back, on the sidelines, or in the shadows. You don't have to be in the spotlight in order to make a difference. But if you have been doing the sacred work of watching, listening, and paying good attention, just know we need more of you in the world. We want to know what you see, hear, and notice. And in the telling, you get to be you. You get to bring your unique contribution in your way.

So if you sense a calling, an invitation, a beckoning to walk into a room, but it feels scary or intimidating, remember the difference between the peace that comes from doing the deeply right thing and the relief that comes from avoidance. There are so many of us here with you. You are not alone.

Finally, be done. Let the last thing end already. If you haven't had a ritual to mark your ending yet, start one. Choose a time to say a specific goodbye. It could be as simple as five minutes of silence or as extravagant as a full weekend of communal toasting. No matter what it is, do a little thinking about how you'll put a period on your endings. And then make it an action, whether it be with a party hat, a toast, a prayer, or a walk. Remember, the goal is not to finish with flair but just to finish. To do it well and to do it fully.

These last few years, as I've navigated the pain of letting go of some things I helped to build, and of the certainty I once had (or thought I had) about God, church, parenting, and more, I've made an imperfect peace with my own endings. Along the way, I'm aware of the temptation to paint past rooms just one shade in my memory, all dark or all light. But this would be unfair and untrue. While I've had moments when I think it would be easier to imagine the church as a villain (both the church we left and the Church as a whole) my friend Jesus will not allow it. I still love and often miss that little church, and I have hope for the global Church we are all part of.

There's more to our story—there always is. There's more to the story of our former church and the things they've navigated since we left that give me hope for what may be to come. We've maintained friendship and connection with several families who still attend, including some who are on staff. We are all learning, growing, and becoming. There's more to all our grief that year than just what I've shared in these pages. And there's more to your story too.

While I've grieved the loss of some of the rooms I've imperfectly exited and felt the growing pains that come with entering new ones, I've been encouraged to learn that when we leave a room, we don't walk into nothing. Something new is always waiting.

As we move forward into all the rooms of our lives, we'll continue to carry the question: "Is it good for me to stay or is it time for me to go?" Sometimes the arrows will point to stay. Other times, they lead us to go. There isn't always a clear answer, and either movement is an act of faith, courage, and patience. Through it all, this will remain: the love of God, the friendship of Jesus, the fellowship of the Spirit, and the beauty of who we are becoming. Together, we'll walk into rooms as our own friend. As we do, we're learning some things along the way.

I'm learning that even though my natural tendency is to lean back and blend in, I'm often called to lean forward.

I'm learning how to bring peace with me into a chaotic situation.

I'm learning how to sit down on the inside even when I have to stand up on the outside.

I'm learning to trust all the ways God shows up around me and within me, and to respond with confidence even in uncertainty.

I'm learning I can be my full, feminine, creative, authentic self and it's not a liability. It's a necessity. A strength. A gift.

I'm learning to access courage to speak up even when it feels unnatural, even when there's opposition, even when I don't want to.

I'm learning I can be a leader even when I'm not in charge. In fact, it's an imperative call.

I don't always remember these things when I walk into rooms, but I'm learning. And it's making a difference.

As much as I sometimes wish it to be otherwise, God is not in the business of making all new things. What God is very much interested in doing is making all the things that already are *all the way new*. Nothing is thrown out. All is being renewed. The kingdom remains strong and unshakable. And the kingdom is in you. So raise your delicate glass of nuance and I'll raise mine too. Together we'll gently toast to beauty and justice as we find a hopeful way forward through the fog.

Our journey has been undergirded with the word "pray" as paths of discernment always must be. As we end our time, I'll borrow a practice of prayer from our Quaker Friends where I'll hold you in the Light.

As you consider the rooms you're in, the rooms you've left, and the rooms you're ready to enter, I will hold you in the Light.

As you evaluate the rooms of your life, as you point to what's true, call it out loud, and consider if it's time to go, I will hold you in the Light.

As you carry the questions those rooms raise in and around you—to apply or not to apply, to accept or decline, to keep trying or to let go, to speak up or to stay quiet, to move on or to dig in—I will hold you in the Light.

As you stand in hallways that seem to have no end, wondering if you have a place to belong, questioning your next right thing, healing from the pain and confusion of goodbyes, I will hold you in the Light.

As you approach new thresholds of possibility, heart full of hope, head full of curiosity, body pulsing with new energy, I will hold you in the Light.

As you navigate all the rooms of your life as the person who you are and are becoming, I will hold you in the Light.

I will hold you in the Light of God who parents us, Christ who befriends us, and Spirit who is our Divine Comfort.

In your arrivals and your departures, may peace be your kind companion, embodying your rooms, following you out, and traveling with you wherever you go.

Amen.

Acknowledgments

This is a book that wanted to arrive within a very specific window of time. I was not ready to write it a day sooner and I'm not sure I could write it now if I had waited any longer. Some books are like that, I guess. Because of the following people, I was able to find these words before it was too late and for that, I offer my heartfelt gratitude. It's an honor to be in the room with you.

Thank you to my literary agent, Lisa Jackson, and the team at Alive for believing in this book from idea to shelf. You make this weird job not feel so weird.

Thank you to the editorial, marketing, sales, and publicity teams at HarperOne, specifically my editor, Katy Hamilton, whose direction and clarity made this book so much better. It's an honor to work with you. And to art director Stephen Brayda, who is pure delight; thank you for making it beautiful.

I continue to be grateful for the expertise and marketing savvy of the team at Unmutable, specifically Caleb and Ana Peavy who offer pastoral professionalism at every turn.

I'm grateful for Team epf, without whom I would be a disorganized puddle on the floor: Mary Freeman, Ashley Sherlock, and

Ginna Neel. Thank you for believing in this work and offering your expertise, creativity, and patience so that we could get it into the hands of the people who need it the most.

I owe a deep measure of gratitude to my fellow spiritual directors in the Anam Cara community as well as the students and colleagues at Friends University, all of whom have taught me what it means to practice a generous orthodoxy.

Bridget Eileen Rivera, thank you for nudging me further.

Thank you to the Olivias. We're saving a seat for you.

To the brilliant women in my two writing groups who have encouraged and affirmed me in this work: Mariah Humphries, Natasha Sistrunk Robinson, Grace Cho, Kat Armas, Shannan Martin, Annie Downs, and Amber Haines. Thank you.

Thank you to my spiritual director, Marion, who has held a sacred space for more than a decade.

Not all rooms have walls and I'm grateful for the virtual spaces where I'm able to gather with readers who subscribe to *The Soul Minimalist* and the listeners of *The Next Right Thing*. Without your questions, curiosity, and support, I would never have written this (or any) book.

A special thank you to Knox McCoy and Jamie B. Golden for your work on *The Popcast* and *The More You Know*, both of which kept me company during nights when I couldn't sleep because I was worried about finishing this book. Your ministry of humor is real and needed.

To my local Lovely Heretics who know what it is to leave rooms that no longer fit: your willingness to hold gracious space is life-giving and, at times, life-saving.

To the friends who listen without trying to solve, you continue to give us courage: Melissa and Randy, Marshall and Diane, and Hannah and Michael. Thank you.

Morland, Smith, Freeman, and Krege families, thank you for your support for and enthusiasm around my work and for always asking how it's going.

To my dear friends, we are the luckiest: Kendra Adachi, thank you for bearing witness to literally everything. I never want to do this work without you. Anna Kimbrough, you've had to leave some beloved rooms way too soon. I'm glad to be in this together with you. Shannan Martin, thank you for wanting all the details and then asking for more. You make staying and leaving not feel so scary.

Thanks to my big sister, Myquillyn, who is on the listening end of every single decision I make in life and work. Please never stop answering your phone.

My deepest gratitude to Ava, Stella, and Luke, who continue to be the most courageous humans I know. The greatest honor of my life is to watch you become who you are. Thank you for believing in us.

John, no matter what room I enter, I'll always be looking for you first. Thank you for rooting for this book and for trusting me to write it.

God our parent, friend, and holy with-ness: thank you for serving as host at the head of the longest table. You are better than we could have ever imagined.

Amen.

As a thank-you for purchasing *How to Walk into a Room*, we have a free gift waiting for you. *Blessings for Hellos and Goodbyes* is an audio companion for you, whether you're leaving a room or entering a new one. Created and read by author Emily P. Freeman, this collection will accompany you through your own rhythms of leaving rooms and finding new ones, narrated by Emily's grounding voice and a reflective, original musical score. To claim your free gift, scan the QR code below and then download *The Quiet Collection* app for iPhone or Android.

www.emilypfreeman.com/blessings

Notes

Part 1. On Leaving: How to Walk out of a Room

1. Pádraig Ó Tuama and Marilyn Nelson, "So Let Us Pick Up the Stones over Which We Stumble, Friends, and Build Altars," interview by Krista Tippett, originally aired September 6, 2018, in *On Being*, podcast, audio, https://onbeing.org/programs/padraig-o-tuama-and-marilyn-nelson-so-let-us-pick-up-the-stones-over-which-we-stumble-friends-and-build-altars/.

Chapter 1: Rooms and Scripts

1. Jeffery R. Young, "Researcher Behind '10,000-Hour Rule' Says Good Teaching Matters, Not Just Practice," May 5, 2020, in *EdSurge*, podcast, audio, 32:29, https://www.edsurge.com/news/2020-05-05-researcher-behind-10-000-hour-rule-says-good-teaching-matters-not-just-practice.

Chapter 2: Point and Call

1. Allan Richarz, "Why Japan's Rail Workers Can't Stop Pointing at Things," Atlas Obscura, March 29, 2017, https://www.atlasobscura.com/articles/pointing-and-calling-japan-trains.

2. James Clear, *Atomic Habits: Tiny Changes, Remarkable Results: An Easy & Proven Way to Build Good Habits and Break Bad Ones* (New York: Avery, 2018), 67.

3. Holly Good, interview by the author, Charlotte, NC, January 15, 2012. "Tiny red flags rarely shrink, they only grow." Years ago when asking for advice about agreeing to a potential speaking event that was proving to be more challenging by the minute, my friend Holly Good said this to me. She cautioned me that if I had a sense that something

was off in the beginning, chances are that by the end, things would have gotten worse. I've found her words continue to ring true, both professionally and personally.

Chapter 3: Identify the Ending

1. "From the Great Resignation to Lying Flat, Workers Are Opting Out," *Bloomberg Businessweek*, December 7, 2021, https://www.bloomberg.com /news/features/2021-12-07/why-people-are-quitting-jobs-and-protesting -work-life-from-the-u-s-to-china.
2. "Why Are Some Chinese Embracing 'Lying Flat'?" interview by Ed Butler, BBC Business Daily, last aired January 19, 2022, audio, 18:00, https://www.bbc.co.uk/programmes/w3ct1jpr#:~:.
3. David Bandurski, "The 'Lying Flat' Movement Standing in the Way of China's Innovation Drive," Brookings, July 8, 2021, https://www .brookings.edu/articles/the-lying-flat-movement-standing-in-the-way-of -chinas-innovation-drive/.

Chapter 4: Remember Your Path

1. Lynn Ungar, "The Path," in *Breathe* (n.p.: Lynn Ungar, 2020), 18. Used with permission.
2. Dallas Willard, *The Divine Conspiracy: Rediscovering Our Hidden Life in God* (San Francisco: HarperSanFrancisco, 1998), 68.
3. Iris Murdoch, *The Sovereignty of Good* (London and New York: Routledge Classics, 1971), 36.
4. Gary Thomas, *Sacred Pathways* (Grand Rapids, MI: Zondervan, 2000), 25.
5. Margaret Silf, *Inner Compass: An Invitation to Ignatian Spirituality* (Chicago: Loyola Press, 1999), 98.
6. Dallas Willard, *The Great Omission* (San Francisco: HarperCollins, 2006).
7. Parker J. Palmer, *Let Your Life Speak* (San Francisco: Jossey-Bass: 2000), 5.
8. "The Inner Life of a Leader," lecture given April 14, 2021 at Friends University.

Chapter 5: Practice Changing Your Mind

1. Page Buono, "Quiet Fire: Indigenous Tribes in California and Other Parts of the US Have Been Rekindling the Ancient Art of Controlled

Burning," The Nature Conservancy, November 2, 2020, https://www
.nature.org/en-us/magazine/magazine-articles/indigenous-controlled
-burns-california/.

2. Sharon McMahon (sharonsaysso), "Anybody who changes their
mind . . ." Instagram Story, March 14, 2022, 2:15 p.m., https://www
.instagram.com/sharonsaysso/.

3. Brian McLaren, "Evolving Faith and Repentance" (speech, Evolving
Faith Conference, Atlanta, GA, October 13, 2022).

4. Robert Bianco, "What USA TODAY Said About the 'Seinfeld' Series
Finale 20 Years Ago," *USA Today*, May 14, 2018, https://www.usatoday
.com/story/life/tv/2018/05/14/seinfeld-finale-20th-anniversary-usa-today
-review/608932002/.

Chapter 6: Arrows and Answers

1. Emily P. Freeman, episode 253, "The Enneagram and Decision-
Making with Suzanne Stabile," November 15, 2022, in *The Next Right
Thing*, podcast, audio, 70:56, https://emilypfreeman.com/podcast/253/.

2. Valerie Brown, "Deep Speaks to Deep: Cultivating Spiritual
Discernment through the Quaker Clearness Committee," *Presence: An
International Journal of Spiritual Direction* Vol. 23, no. 4 (December
2017): 20, https://www.valeriebrown.us/wp-content/uploads/2014/12
/Deep-Speaks-to-Deep-Cultivating-Spiritual-Discernment-through-the
-Quaker-Clearness-Committee.pdf

3. "The Russell Moore Show: Beth Moore Didn't Expect Us to Be Us,"
posted October 7, 2021, Christianity Today, YouTube video of podcast,
60:00, https://www.youtube.com/watch?v=_YJlWWMz_wA.

4. Bridget Eileen Rivera, *Heavy Burdens: Seven Ways LGBTQ Christians
Experience Harm in the Church* (Grand Rapids, MI: Brazos Press, 2021),
Back cover.

5. "2022 National Survey on LGBTQ Youth Mental Health," The Trevor
Project, https://www.thetrevorproject.org/survey-2022/#intro.

6. Centers for Disease Control and Prevention, *Youth Risk Behavior Survey
Data Summary & Trends Report: 2011–2021*, February 13, 2023, https://
www.cdc.gov/healthyyouth/data/yrbs/pdf/YRBS_Data-Summary-Trends
_Report2023_508.pdf.

7. N. T. Wright DD FRSE, University of St. Andrews, Calvin College
January Series, January 24, 2017, https://ntwrightpage.com/2017/01/30
/the-royal-revolution-fresh-perspectives-on-the-cross/.

8. Barbara Brown Taylor, *Learning to Walk in the Dark* (San Francisco: HarperOne, 2014), 129.

Chapter 7: Peace or Avoidance

1. Amanda Gorman, *The Hill We Climb* (New York: Penguin Random House, 2021), 3.
2. Emily P. Freeman, episode 213, "How to Make Embodied Decisions with Dr. Hillary L. McBride," February 15, 2022, in *The Next Right Thing*, podcast, audio, 36:18, https://emilypfreeman.com/podcast/213/.
3. Emily Nagoski and Amelia Nagoski, *Burnout: The Secret to Unlocking the Stress Cycle* (New York: Ballantine, 2019), 27.

Chapter 8: Readiness or Timeliness

1. "Creating Saturday Night Live: Film Unit," produced by Lorne Michaels et al., posted April 22, 2019, *Saturday Night Live*, YouTube video, 12:40, https://www.youtube.com/watch?v=FXJKfK_aMDI.
2. Tina Fey, *Bossypants* (New York: Little, Brown, 2011), 123.
3. Christie Purifoy, *Placemaker* (Grand Rapids, MI: Zondervan, 2019), 46.

Chapter 9: Endings and Closure

1. C. S. Lewis, *C. S. Lewis Letters to Children*, ed. Lyle W. Dorsett and Marjorie Lamp Mead (New York: Simon & Schuster, 1995), 64.
2. Ronald Rolheiser, *The Holy Longing: The Search for a Christian Spirituality* (New York: Doubleday, 1999), 62.
3. Madeleine L'Engle, *A Circle of Quiet* (New York: Farrar, Straus and Giroux, 1972), 199–200.

Chapter 10: Walk in as a Leader

1. Rania Aniftos, "Claudia Conway Wants to 'Get Out of the Drama,' Auditions for 'American Idol,'" *Billboard*, February 15, 2021, https://www.billboard.com/music/music-news/claudia-conway-american-idol-9526277/.
2. Edwin H. Friedman, *A Failure of Nerve: Leadership in the Age of the Quick Fix*, ed. Margaret M. Treadwell, and Edward W. Beal (New York: New York, 2017), 15–16.
3. Friedman, *A Failure of Nerve*, 29.
4. Barbara Brown Taylor, *Leaving Church: A Memoir of Faith* (San Francisco: HarperSanFrancisco, 2007), 81.

5. Brian Zahnd, *When Everything's on Fire* (Downers Grove, IL: InterVarsity Press, 2021), 46.

Chapter 11: Walk in as a Listener

1. Tara M. Owens, *Embracing the Body* (Downers Grove, IL: InterVarsity Press, 2015), 59.

Chapter 12: Walk in as Your Own Friend

1. Johnathan Strickland, "How the Apollo Spacecraft Worked," How Stuff Works, March 10, 2008, https://science.howstuffworks.com/apollo -spacecraft7.htm.